Concerto for Two Pianos and Orchestra in E Major (1823)

Recent Researches in Music

A-R Editions publishes seven series of critical editions, spanning the history of Western music, American music, and oral traditions.

Recent Researches in the Music of the Middle Ages and Early Renaissance
   Charles M. Atkinson, general editor

Recent Researches in the Music of the Renaissance
   James Haar, general editor

Recent Researches in the Music of the Baroque Era
   Christoph Wolff, general editor

Recent Researches in the Music of the Classical Era
   Eugene K. Wolf, general editor

Recent Researches in the Music of the Nineteenth and Early Twentieth Centuries
   Rufus Hallmark, general editor

Recent Researches in American Music
   John M. Graziano, general editor

Recent Researches in the Oral Traditions of Music
   Philip V. Bohlman, general editor

Each edition in *Recent Researches* is devoted to works by a single composer or to a single genre. The content is chosen for its high quality and historical importance, and each edition includes a substantial introduction and critical report. The music is engraved according to the highest standards of production using the proprietary software MusE, owned by Music|Notes.™

For information on establishing a standing order to any of our series, or for editorial guidelines on submitting proposals, please contact:

A-R Editions, Inc.
801 Deming Way
Madison, Wisconsin 53717

800 736-0070 (U.S. book orders)
608 836-9000 (phone)
608 831-8200 (fax)
http://www.areditions.com

RECENT RESEARCHES IN THE MUSIC OF THE NINETEENTH AND EARLY TWENTIETH CENTURIES, 28

Felix Mendelssohn

Concerto for Two Pianos and Orchestra in E Major (1823)

Original Version of the First Movement

Edited by Stephan D. Lindeman

A-R Editions, Inc.
Madison

For Douglas Johnson

A-R Editions, Inc., Madison, Wisconsin 53717
© 1999 by A-R Editions, Inc.

All rights reserved. No part of this book may be reproduced or transmitted in any form by any electronic or mechanical means (including photocopying, recording, or information storage and retrieval) without permission in writing from the publisher.

The purchase of this work does not convey the right to perform it in public, nor to make a recording of it for any purpose. Such permission must be obtained in advance from the publisher.

A-R Editions is pleased to support scholars and performers in their use of *Recent Researches* material for study or performance. Subscribers to any of the *Recent Researches* series, as well as patrons of subscribing institutions, are invited to apply for information about our "Copyright Sharing Policy."

Printed in the United States of America

ISBN 0-89579-439-X
ISSN 0193-5364

∞ The paper used in this publication meets the minimum requirements of the American National Standard for Information Sciences—Permanence of Paper for Printed Library Materials, ANSI Z39.48-1984.

Contents

Acknowledgments vi

Introduction vii
  Context viii
  Mendelssohn's Concerto for Two Pianos and Orchestra in E Major ix
  Performances and Reception x
  Notes xiii

Plates xv

Concerto for Two Pianos and Orchestra in E Major 1

Critical Report 113
  Sources 113
  Editorial Method 113
  Critical Notes 115
  Notes 117

Acknowledgments

I acknowledge and extend a sincere thank you to the following colleagues and friends for their assistance in the creation of this edition: Murray Boren, Ed Cedar, Ruth Fries-Robbins, Walter Frisch, Clifford Gilmore, Floyd K. Grave, Rufus Hallmark, Ingeborg Heussner, the late Theodore Hunt, the late Elizabeth Ann Kessinger, Sharon Kessinger, Rick Koenig, Karl-Heinz Köhler, C. Steven LaRue, Timothy H. Lindeman, Michael Minch, Joseph Orchard, Ellen Rosand, James Scott, Floyd G. Sumner, Ronald M. Surak, R. Larry Todd, Ron Wiecki, and James Worley.

I was assisted greatly by the following libraries and institutions, and their respective staffs: the Deutsche Staatsbibliothek zu Berlin Preußischer Kulturbesitz, Musikabteilung mit Mendelssohn Archiv: Eveline Bartlitz, Birgit Busse, Arnim Eisenach, Wolfgang Goldhan, Helmut Hell, Hans-Günter Klein, and Frank Ziegler; the Blanche and Irving Laurie Music Library, and other Libraries of Rutgers University, New Brunswick, NJ: Roger Tarman, Phyllis Palfy, Harriette Hemmasi, Ingeborg Heussner, Glenn Sandberg, Arlene Pelayo, Ines Gessner, Robert Terrio, Kenneth Yarmey, Manny Servio, Gracemary Smulewitz, Michel Tokar, Andre Andrew, and Melody Tomaszewicz; the Bodleian Library, Oxford University: Peter A. Ward Jones and Melissa Dalziel; and the *Leipziger Ausgabe der Werke Felix Mendelssohn Bartholdys*: Ralf Wehner.

I am indebted to generous grants funded by the Mason Gross School of the Arts, Department of Music, Rutgers University, and the College of Fine Arts and Communications, Brigham Young University.

I am particularly grateful to Douglas Johnson for his help and guidance.

Introduction

Felix Mendelssohn (1809–47) wrote the Concerto for Two Pianos and Orchestra in E major in the late summer and early autumn of 1823, when he was fourteen years old (see plate 1). The work stems from a time in his development when he was beginning to explore the larger forms, as manifested in such works as the twelve string symphonias (composed during the years 1821–23), sacred works including the Psalm lxvi and the D major Magnificat (both from 1822), the two Singspiels *Die wandernden Komödianten* (1821–22) and *Der Onkel aus Boston oder Die beiden Neffen* (1822–23), and four other concertos, for various instruments (1822–24).[1]

Mendelssohn dated the completion of the first movement of the autograph manuscript of the Concerto for Two Pianos and Orchestra in E major *d. 13ten Sept. 1823* (see plate 2).[2] The second movement is not dated; the third is inscribed *d. 17 Oct. 1823*. These dates bespeak a feverish rate of composition, entirely consistent with the rapid production of other works during 1823. During this year alone, Mendelssohn composed a Concerto for Violin, Piano, and Strings in D minor (the composer's third concerto attempt, following a Concerto for Violin and Strings in D minor, and a Concerto for Piano and Strings in A minor, both from 1822), five string sinfonias, a comic opera (his sixth dramatic work), a Kyrie for solo voices and double chorus, a string quartet, a violin sonata, a piano sonata, a piano quartet, two little pieces for organ, and a number of songs.[3]

Both the E major Concerto for Two Pianos and Orchestra, and its companion piece, the later A-flat major Concerto for Two Pianos and Orchestra (the last of the five early concertos attempted during the years 1822–24, and completed just over a year after the E major concerto, in November 1824), were written as birthday presents for Felix's older sister Fanny (born 14 November 1805).[4] The E major concerto was first performed during early December 1823, as part of the Mendelssohn family's Sunday *musicales* in their Berlin home, with the two siblings as soloists.[5] For these concerts, whatever musicians were needed (sometimes an entire orchestra) were hired by the Mendelssohns in order to fully instruct Fanny and Felix in the proper handling of all the instruments. This is how the children learned firsthand the crafts of orchestration, conducting, and rehearsal technique.

The composer and pianist Ignaz Moscheles played an important role in the preservation of the Mendelssohn Concerto for Two Pianos and Orchestra in E major in its original version. Born in Prague in 1794, he lived in Vienna from 1808 until 1825, where he studied with Salieri and Albrechtsberger, and became close with Beethoven. In 1825, he moved to London, where he taught at the Royal Academy of Music (teaching Litolff and Thalberg), and was a conductor of the Philharmonic Society. He moved to Leipzig in 1846 at Mendelssohn's request to head the piano area at the newly formed Leipzig Conservatory. He died in Leipzig in 1870.

Moscheles was, in the early 1820s, one of the most highly regarded composers and virtuosos in the world. In the midst of a lengthy European continental tour as a recitalist, he spent most of November and December 1824 in Berlin, en route to Paris and London from Vienna. At this time, the Mendelssohn's had established their Berlin home as an artistic and intellectual center of the city's leading artists, musicians, and intellectuals. It was typical for persons of note traveling through Berlin to visit the Mendelssohn home ("thronged with the intellect and wit of Berlin"),[6] participate in the frequent music making, and dine with the family. Guests included Ludwig Berger, Heinrich Heine, Alexander and Wilhelm von Humbolt, Johann Nepomuk Hummel, Frédéric Kalkbrenner, Bernhard Klein, Louis Spohr, Carl Maria von Weber, Carl Friedrich Zelter, and many others.

Moscheles was thirty years old at the time of his visit to Berlin. His diary provides few details of his overall visit to the city.[7] In sharp contrast, however, it is filled with pages of details concerning his almost daily visits to the Mendelssohn home, his impressions of the fifteen-year-old Felix, nineteen-year-old Fanny, their parents, performances by the two siblings, and his rather reluctant "teaching" of Felix, due to the latter's almost complete artistic maturity. Felix performed or showed Moscheles the manuscripts of several of his compositions, including a double concerto. Moscheles was so impressed with these works ("Felix ... is a phenomenon ... already a mature artist")[8] that he copied out the score of the Concerto for Two Pianos and Orchestra in E major in his own hand (see plate 3).[9] This copy is extant, and helps to corroborate and clarify a number of important discrepancies in the Mendelssohn autograph manuscript. No other sources or sketch materials for the work survive.[10]

The two subsequently became close friends and colleagues. During Mendelssohn's first visit to London five years later, Mendelssohn and Moscheles performed the Concerto for Two Pianos and Orchestra in E major from manuscript. This concert, Mendelssohn's fourth in London, was given in the Argyll Rooms (site of the Philharmonic concerts) on 13 July 1829. The concert was organized by Mendelssohn's Uncle Nathan (perhaps jointly with the singer Henriette Sontag) in order to benefit the victims of floods in Silesia.[11] The Overture to *A Midsummer Night's Dream* was also performed during this concert.

Probably in preparation for this performance, Mendelssohn substantially revised the concerto, particularly the first movement. His autograph score is filled with many cross outs, revisions, alterations, and directions, in English, most likely intended for the conductor of the 1829 performance. He may have continued the revision process as late as 1833, in preparation for his third visit to London in the spring of that year, as a result of a letter from Moscheles at that time requesting that he bring one of the two double concertos for them to perform.[12]

Like the four other concertos composed during the years 1822–24, which were not published in Mendelssohn's life time, the highly self-critical composer chose to publish neither the original, nor the revised version of the Concerto for Two Pianos and Orchestra in E major. The heavily revised version of the first movement, with approximately twenty percent of the original removed, and substantial portions of the remaining portions altered, was first published only in 1960 by the *Leipziger Ausgabe der Werke Felix Mendelssohn Bartholdys*, edited by Karl-Heinz Köhler.[13]

Only three nineteenth-century performances are known: the premiere with Fanny in December 1823, the 1829 performance in London with Moscheles, and a performance by two of Moscheles's students at the Leipzig Conservatory in 1860 (see plate 4).[14]

Study of this early (first) version of the Concerto for Two Pianos and Orchestra in E major is important because it provides a view into Mendelssohn's compositional workshop. By comparing the first version with the revised concerto published in the Leipziger Ausgabe, we can gain many important insights into Mendelssohn's technical and aesthetic development as a composer.

Context

All of Mendelssohn's five early concertos were written following the model of the Mozart piano concertos (with first movements in "double-exposition" form),[15] whose style Mendelssohn had studied in detail during the years 1819 to 1821.[16] All the Mozart piano concertos are cast in three movements, typically consisting of an opening allegro, a subsequent slow movement, and a rondo or sonata-rondo finale. The first movements employ double exposition form cast in seven parts and defined in part by tutti / solo contrast, as well as the procedures of sonata form. These seven parts consist of:
1) Ritornello 1 (tutti exposition)
2) Solo exposition
3) Ritornello 2
4) Development
5) Recapitulation
6) a. Tutti statement leading to cadenza (where relevant)
   b. Cadenza (sometimes omitted)
7) Ritornello 3[17]

Sir Donald Francis Tovey offered as a *locus classicus* of his "concerto principle"[18] the first movement of Mozart's Piano Concerto no. 25 in C major, K. 503 (composed in Vienna, and completed on 4 December 1786).[19] Using the thematic shorthand suggested in Jan LaRue's *Guidelines for Style Analysis*[20] (P = primary thematic material; T = areas of transition; S = secondary theme; K = closing material; digressions are areas of tonal instability), and following a model developed by Douglas Johnson, I have constructed the following schematic diagram, hereafter referred to as a *time line* to show how Tovey's model works in this movement (see table 1).[21] The movement consists of three main ritornelli framing two solo sections: R^1 (R = ritornello) is the tutti exposition, subsequently followed by the solo exposition; the second ritornello closes the solo exposition and leads to the development; the second solo section constitutes the development and the recapitulation; R^3 rounds out the recapitulation. All of the Mozart piano concertos (except no. 1, K. 37) call for an improvised cadenza to display even further the soloist's capabilities, both as an improviser and as a virtuoso.

In the early years of the nineteenth century, the next generation of composers working in the concerto genre continued to exploit the possibilities inherent in the form as perfected in the great Mozart concertos, all twenty-three of which had been published by 1806.[22] Mozart's student, Johann Nepomuk Hummel (1778–1837), wrote a number of concertos that were highly influential on the composers of Mendelssohn's generation. One of these, the Piano Concerto in A minor, op. 85 (published ca. 1816), was in the repertoire of Franz Liszt, Robert Schumann, and Clara Wieck. Mendelssohn scholar Marian Wilson has shown how Felix Mendelssohn modeled his very first attempt in the genre, the Concerto for Piano and Strings in A minor (composed two years before the E major Concerto, in 1821), on Hummel's op. 85.[23] A time line of this work is presented in table 2.

All of Hummel's concertos essentially follow the Mozartian pattern. However, Hummel's op. 85 differs from his teacher's works in a number of areas. For example, much greater technical demands are placed on the soloist. This is seen towards the climax of the solo exposition, just before the onset of the second ritornello, and in the recapitulation, at the comparable position. Moreover, no improvised cadenza is called for. And lastly, op. 85 contains many colorful juxtapositions of distantly related sonorities, infusing a rich harmonic color. For example, the development begins abruptly with a shift from E major to C major, a chromatic mediant relationship. Relationships of this kind are generally found much less frequently in Mozart's concertos, and are a common element in the works of the early Romantics.

TABLE 1
Mozart, Piano Concerto in C major, K. 503 (1786), first movement

Ritornello 1			Solo Exposition			Recapitulation	
			Solo entry (new)		92–112		
P^1		1–15	P^1 tutti		112–26	P^1 tutti/solo	290–303
P^2 I–i–V		15–26	P^2 (varied) I–i–V		126–46	P^2	304–24
T^1 I–V		26–44	T^2 (new) ♭III–V/V		146–70	T^2 ♭III–V	324–45
confirm V		44–51					
S^1 i–♭III–i		51–59	S^2 (new) in V		170–78	S^2 in I	345–53
S^1 varied repeat in I		59–66	S^2 tutti repeat		178–87	S^2 repeat	353–65
						S^1 in I	365–72
K^1 in I		66–82	K^3 (new) in V		187–98	K^3 in I	372–82
K^2		82–91	K^3 varied repeat, to			K^3 to V–I solo to	
			V/V–V solo trills		198–214	V–I solo trills	382–99
merge with solo entrance		91–96					
			Ritornello 2			**Tutti leads to Cadenza**	
			T^1 varied in V		214–28	T^1 varied	399–410
			to V/e (iii/I)		228–31	Cadenza	410–11
			Development			**Ritornello 3**	
			material	*key*		K^1 in I	411–23
						K^2 in I	423–32
			S^1	e–a–G–g	231–61		
			S^1 in canon	a ~ V/I	261–90		

Like Hummel, Moscheles initially followed the Mozart pattern, as witnessed in his Piano Concerto no. 2 in E-flat major, op. 56, a work which Mendelssohn heard Moscheles perform in Berlin at their first meeting in 1824, and which impressed him profoundly.[24] A time line of this work is presented in table 3.

Moscheles takes his cue from Hummel, and places even more challenging virtuosic demands on the soloist. Perhaps of greater interest is the degree to which the harmonic palette of this concerto has been enriched. Notice that after the statement of the S^2 group in the exposition and recapitulation, Moscheles inserts a cyclic harmonic digression. This digression propels the harmonic motion far away from its intended goal (the dominant at the end of the exposition, and the tonic in the recapitulation), with a prolongation of the distant area of the flat submediant. And like Hummel, Moscheles calls for no improvised cadenza.

Hummel's and Moscheles's advances were not lost on the adolescent Mendelssohn. The young firebrand's E major concerto for two pianos is replete with pyrotechnical passages for the soloists, and harmonic digressions to distant areas. Moreover, no cadenza was included in the original version. Perhaps again following the lead of Hummel and Moscheles, the E major concerto is also the first which Mendelssohn scored for a modern orchestra, including brass, winds, and drums (all of the symphonias are orchestrated for strings only, as are the three concertos which precede the E major Concerto). The work thus represents a significant stride in his development as a composer. The lessons learned in this, and the other large-scale works composed during the early 1820s—primarily the five concertos, and the string symphonias—resulted in Mendelssohn's first two undisputed masterpieces, the Octet for Strings, op. 20 (composed in 1825), and the Overture to *A Midsummer Night's Dream*, op. 21 (1826). Moreover, Mendelssohn realized, through his attempts in the concerto genre with such works as the E major concerto, that the double-exposition form was too rooted in the classical style. His three mature concertos following in the wake of the five early concertos—the Piano Concerto no. 1 in G minor, op. 25 (composed in 1831 and published in 1832), the Piano Concerto no. 2 in D minor, op. 40 (composed in 1837 and published in 1838), and the Violin Concerto in E minor, op. 64 (composed in 1844 and published in 1845)—are all cast in a radically new design, primarily of his own invention. These works all feature, in varying degrees, a combined tutti and solo exposition, lack of improvised cadenzas, seamless transitions between movements, and thematic connections between movements, creating a more cohesive and organic formal design.

Mendelssohn's Concerto for Two Pianos and Orchestra in E major

Table 4 presents a time line of the first movement of the Mendelssohn concerto. As is evident, the work is cast in fairly regular double-exposition form. It shimmers with virtuosic passages, tossed back and forth between the two soloists. At the beginning of the development, the abrupt initial step to a key a major third lower than the expected

TABLE 2
Hummel, Piano Concerto in A minor, op. 85 (ca. 1816), first movement

Ritornello 1		Solo Exposition			Recapitulation	
P^1	1–9	enter on V		120–24	P^1 tutti	369–75
P^2	10–20	flourish on i		124–31	P^2 solo	376–83
		P^2		132–39		
		confirms i		139–52		
$T^1 = P^1$ to V/III	20–49	$T^1 = P^1$ varied & extension, to V/III		153–84	T^2 (new; brief) to V/I	383–94
S^1 in III	50–58	S^1 in III		185–93	S^1 in I	395–403
S^2	58–65	S^2		193–200	S^2	403–10
$S^3 = P^2$ in III	66–72	$S^3 = P^2$ in III		201–11	S^3	411–28
S^2 repeat	73–78	cadential material		211–23	exposition varied cadenza-like, to	428–48
retransition–V/i	79–87	digression = cyclic modulation to solo V/III trills		223–57	solo V/i trills	449–65
$K^1 = P^2$ i	88–99	**Ritornello 2**			**Ritornello 3**	
K^2 back to i	99–104					
K^4 repeat beginning, resolve to N♭II–V	105–11	P^1 varied, in III		257–71	confirms i (new)	465–71
		P^2 in III		272–82		
prepare solo entrance	111–19	prepare solo entrance, like R^1, to E (V/A)		283–89		
		Development				
		material	*key*			
		solo arpeggios	E, immediately change to V/C	289–22		
		solo, new (?)	C	293–300		
		P^2	C	301–38		
		cyclic	B♭–E♭–A♭–D♭– f♯–c♯–a♭–e♭– d♯°–V/i	308–38		

tone of resolution (a deceptive resolution, V/B to G major) was something that had become increasingly common in early romantic works. There is only one example in the first movements of the Mozart piano concertos (no. 17 in G major, K. 453, composed in 1784) and one in Beethoven (Piano Concerto no. 4 in G major, op. 58, composed 1805–06), but it is found in Carl Maria von Weber's Piano Concerto no. 1 in C Major (published in 1810), Hummel's Piano Concerto in B minor, op. 89 (published ca. 1819), and Moscheles's Piano Concerto no. 3 in G minor, op. 60 (also published as op. 58, ca. 1820), among many others. This striking tonal relationship seems to have especially enamored the young Mendelssohn during these years. It is present in a number of works from this period, including his first published work, the Piano Quartet no. 1 in C minor, op. 1 (composed in 1822) (the development initially moves from E-flat minor to B major [enharmonic C♭]), the Piano Quartet no. 2 in F minor, op. 2 (composed in 1823) (the development progresses sequentially B-flat minor to F-sharp major, B minor to G major, and C minor to A-flat major), and the Concerto for Violin and Piano in D minor, also composed in 1823, where the beginning of the development shifts dramatically from F major to D-flat major.[25]

As mentioned above, Mendelssohn substantially revised the first movement, probably for the 1829 London performance, and perhaps in 1833 as well. At one point during the revision process, Mendelssohn contemplated the excision of some 90 measures, about 20% of the movement (originally 453 measures), though he later restored or recomposed two of these deletions. A linear reduction graph in my study published in *Musical Quarterly* illustrates Mendelssohn's revisions. He had second thoughts, however, and evidently intended to restore a number of passages, as is evident from the instructions "Stet," "In," "This," and "Not This" on manuscript pages 52 through 55 (see plate 6).[26]

Performances and Reception

As noted above, the E major concerto received its premiere with Felix and Fanny as soloists during the first

TABLE 3
Moscheles, Piano Concerto no. 2 in E-flat major, op. 56 (ca. 1825), first movement

Ritornello 1		**Solo Exposition**		**Recapitulation**	
P^1	1–18	P^1 varied	69–79	P^1 tutti	265–82
T^1 I–V/V–V	18–26	P^1 varied repeat = T2 I–big V/V	79–99	[omit T]	
		V/V prolongation to digression	100-16		
S^1 V–I	27–30	S^1 in V	117–25	S^1 solo in I	282–90
S^1 varied repeat–g	31–34	S^1 continued	126–47	S^1 continued	290–98
S^1 varied repeat	35–38	S^2 group (new) in V	147–55	[omit S^2 group]	
S^1 varied repeat	39–42	digression to G♭; to V/III–III solo trills	155–94	digression to C♭; to V/i–i solo trills	298–341
I-brief digression–V^7	42–56				
K^1 varied repeat/ extension	62–68	**Ritornello 2**		**Ritornello 3**	
$K^1 = P^1$ varied to I	57–61	P^1 reference V–g	194–219	P^1 new varied	341–52
		Development	[no cadenza]		
		material	*key*		
		P^1	g (vi/V)	219–29	
		arpeggios/scalar	d–e–f♯–a–d– E♭–G	229–47	
		S^1	G (quite prolonged)	248–62	
		abrupt shift	g–V/I (retransition)	262–64	

Source: *Concerto für das Pianoforte . . . op. 56* (Vienna: Carl Haslinger q^d Tobias; Berlin: Schlesinger [n.d.]); print in US-Bc. Another edition: *No. 2 Grosses Concert . . .* (Vienna: S. A. Steiner & Comp., n.d. [1826?]), plate no. S:u:C 4613; print in US-NYp.

---

week of December 1823. The next documented performance is the London performance with Moscheles in July 1829.[27] At least seven accounts of this concert survive: a letter from Mendelssohn to his father, another to his Uncle Nathan, two reports by Mendelssohn's and Moscheles's friend, Carl Klingemann (who knew Mendelssohn in Berlin, and was attached to the Hanoverian embassy in London), an anonymous article in the *Berliner allgemeine musikalische Zeitung*, a review of the concert in *The Harmonicon*, and an account in the diary of Moscheles.[28]

The most interesting account is the composer's letter to his father of 10 July, written three days before the concert. It provides an amusing description of Mendelssohn's and Moscheles's first rehearsal of the concerto at the Clementi piano factory in London.

> Yesterday we had our first rehearsal at the Clementi factory . . . I had no end of fun; for you cannot imagine how we coquetted; how the one constantly imitated the other and how sweet we were. Moscheles plays the last movement with remarkable brilliance; he shook the runs out of his sleeve. When it was over everyone said it was such a shame that we hadn't played any cadenzas, so I at once dug up a place in the final tutti of the first movement where the orchestra has a fermata, and Moscheles was prevailed upon *nolens volens* to compose a big cadenza; we then tried to figure out, meanwhile making a thousand pranks, whether the last little solo (*vide Fanny*) could be left as was, since people would no doubt applaud. We need a little tutti between the cadenza and the final solo, I said. How long are they supposed to applaud? asked Moscheles. Ten minutes, I dare say, said I. Moscheles bargained me down to five. I promised to provide a tutti, and so we took proper measurements, patched, turned, and padded things together, stitched on some sleeves à la Mameluke, and tailored a brilliant concerto. Today there is another rehearsal, it will be quite a musical picnic, for Moscheles is bringing the cadenza along [see plate 5], and I the tutti.[29]

The only other documented performance in the nineteenth century occurred over thirty years later. On 22 June 1860, some twelve and a half years after Felix Mendelssohn's death, Moscheles attended an informal evening of music at the Leipzig Conservatory of Music, where he was a Professor of Piano. At this event, two of his students, Natalie Schilling and Bertha Schwalbe, played the Concerto in E major.[30] Moscheles noted the event in his diary and in an inscription he scribbled on the cover of a manuscript copy of the concerto that he himself had copied decades earlier, which his students

TABLE 4
Felix Mendelssohn, Concerto for Two Pianos and Orchestra in E major (1823), first movement

Ritornello 1		Soli Exposition		Recapitulation	
P¹	1–16	P² soli flourish	88–103	P²	322–36 [264–78]
		[cross out 6 mm.: P¹ fugal]	103–108	[P¹ omitted; 26 mm. T material crossed out (mm. 336–61 [278–303]), then restored]	
		tutti confirm I	109–111 [103–105]*		
T¹ I–V/V	16–28	T² (new) I–V/i	111–26 [105–20]	T¹ tutti I–V/i	336–48 [278–90]
digression V/V–♮VII (D)–♮III (G)–V/V	28–43	digression V–♮III (G)–V/V	126–38 [120–32]	digression V–♮III (G)–V	348–60 [290–302]
S in V	44–52	S in V	138–46 [132–40]	S in I	360–68 [302–10]
S varied repeat in v	52–57	S varied repeat in V	146–51 [140–45]	S varied repeat in I	368–73 [310–15]
deceptive resolution to C (♮VI)	58–61	deceptive resolution to ♮III (G)–V/V	152–53 [146–47]	deceptive resolution to ♮VI (C)–V	374–75 [316–17]
transition to V/I	62–75	transition to V/V	154–61 [148–55]	transition to V/I	376–80 [318–22]
P¹ varied = K I–V⁷	76–87	K² (new) in V	161–69 [155–63]	K² in I	381–89 [323–31]
		K³ in V	169–73 [163–67]	K³ in I	389–93 [331–35]
		[cross out 10 mm.: 4 mm. V–V/V; 6 mm. I–N♮II–vii°/iii–vii°/IV–IV–V]	173–82		
		P¹ fugal = K⁴ in V, to V/V–V solo trills	183–210 [167–94]	K⁴ in I to V	393–413 [335–55]
				P¹ tutti/ soli, I	414–32 [356–74]
		Ritornello 2		**Ritornello 3**	
		T¹ in V–v–V/v	211–22 [195–206]	T¹ in I	432–37 [374–79]
		[cross out 16 mm.: 8 mm. in V + 8 mm. transition to V/G]	223–38	Cadenza	437 [379]
		Revision creates a deceptive resolution to G (♮III)	[207]	Coda tutti/soli	438–50 [380–92]
		Development			
		material *key*			
		P² G	239–47 [207–15]		
		transition b	247–55 [215–23]		
		tutti confirm b	255–57 [223–25]		
		T² b–f#–c#–f#–b–E–A–a–e–B	257–81 [225–49]		
		[cross out 37 mm.: P¹ fugal in D–G–C–D, and T¹ in D–G; replaced in later revisions by one brief statement of S in V]	279–312		
		S [in revision] B	281–86; 313 [249–55]		
		V preparation V/I	287–321 [255–63]		

* Measure numbers of Köhler edition in brackets.

used for this performance (see plate 4).[31] In his diary, he noted: "It was interesting to hear how the 14-year-old Mendelssohn had composed like Mozart. In the Program Book, I listed it as by F. Knospe."[32]

Moscheles seems to be having a bit of fun here by creating a pun on the noun "Knospe" (bud)—implying that the concerto was the work of a "budding" composer. The fact that Moscheles had by then apparently forgotten Mendelssohn's attempts to turn the concerto into something more mature had the unintended result, it seems, of returning it to its original state. It is left for us to wonder whether, in the end, Mendelssohn might have preferred to leave it that way, too: not as a mature work of art which he intended to publish, but as a reminder of the great promise the adolescent composer held in the early 1820s, and which was brought to fruition in the Octet, the *Midsummer Night's Dream* and *Hebrides* Overtures, the symphonies, the two piano concertos, opp. 25 and 40, and the Violin Concerto in E minor, op. 64.

Notes

1. See R. Larry Todd, *Mendelssohn's Musical Education: A Study and Edition of his Exercises in Composition* (Cambridge: Cambridge University Press, 1983). See also *The New Grove Dictionary of Music and Musicians* (6th ed.), s.v., "Mendelssohn, Felix," by Karl-Heinz Köhler, 135–36 (work list by Eveline Bartlitz, 152–53) (hereafter cited as NG "Mendelssohn"); repr. in *The New Grove Early Romantic Masters 2*, rev. R. Larry Todd (New York: W. W. Norton, 1985), 270–83 (hereafter cited as Todd, *Early Romantic Masters*). Köhler describes a phase of ripening maturity in Mendelssohn's youthful evolution, beginning in the wake of his first visit with Johann Wolfgang von Goethe in Weimar in November 1821. This visit was arranged by Mendelssohn's composition teacher, Carl Friedrich Zelter, a close friend of Goethe.

2. Felix Mendelssohn, Concerto for Two Pianos and Orchestra in E major, Staatsbibliothek zu Berlin Preußischer Kulturbesitz, Musikabteilung mit Mendelssohn Archiv (hereafter cited as D-B Mendelssohn Archiv), Mus. ms. MN 15.

3. NG "Mendelssohn," work list; revised in Todd, *Early Romantic Masters*, 272.

4. Eric Werner, "Two Unpublished Mendelssohn Concertos," *Music and Letters* 36 (1955): 129.

5. Rudolf Elvers, ed., *Felix Mendelssohn: A Life in Letters*, trans. Craig Tomlinson (New York: Fromm International, 1986), 18 (hereafter cited as *Mendelssohn Letters*, ed. Elvers). Bartlitz and Todd are apparently in error here, listing 14 November 1824 as the date of the first performance; see the work list in NG "Mendelssohn," 153 and *Early Romantic Masters*, 272.

6. *A Dictionary of Music and Musicians* (1st ed.), s.v., "Mendelssohn, Felix," by Sir George Grove. Felix and Fanny were both born in Hamburg. The Mendelssohn family moved to Berlin in 1811, shortly after the birth of their third child, Rebecka (11 April 1811). They remained in their Berlin home at no. 7 Neue Promenade, in what was at that time the northeast quarter of the city, until 1825, when they moved to no. 3 Leipzigerstraße. This house remained in the family until after the death of Fanny in 1847.

7. Charlotte Moscheles, ed., *Aus Moscheles's Leben* (Leipzig, 1872); adapted from the German by A. D. Coleridge under the title *Recent Music and Musicians: As Described in the Diaries and Correspondence of Ignatz [sic] Moscheles* (New York: Henry Holt, 1873; repr. New York: Da Capo, 1970), 65–68.

8. Ibid., 65.

9. Manuscript copy in the hand of Ignaz Moscheles of the Felix Mendelssohn Concerto for Two Pianos and Orchestra in E major, D-B Mendelssohn Archiv, Mus. ms. 14325/4. Shelved with the MS score is a set of undated string parts, in a copyist's hand, copied from the score. As Moscheles' copy is not dated, it is not certain that he copied the work at this time (1824). The subsequent history of the work implies that this was the time that he copied it, however.

10. A corollary manuscript to the Mendelssohn autograph and the Moscheles copy survives in the hand of Ignaz Moscheles (see plate 5). It is a cadenza to the first movement for Piano 1, preserved among the Mendelssohn Papers in the Bodleian Library, Oxford; see *Catalogue of the Mendelssohn Papers in the Bodleian Library, Oxford*, vol. 2: *Music and Papers*, compiled by Margaret Crum (Tutzing: Hans Schneider, 1980), 4: "C. 86: Ignaz Moscheles, loose sheets of music. Bequeathed by Helena Deneke, 1973: no. 3: F.M.B.'s cadenza for concerto for 2 pianos in E, 1823 (MS. Them. Cat. p. 24)." This is apparently the cadenza to which Mendelssohn referred in his letter of 10 July 1829 to his father, which Moscheles brought to their "musical picnic." For more on the circumstances surrounding the performance of the Concerto for Two Pianos and Orchestra in E Major by Mendelssohn and Moscheles in London in 1829, see Stephan D. Lindeman, "Mendelssohn and Moscheles: Two Composers, Two Pianos, Two Scores, One Concerto," *Musical Quarterly* 83 (1999): 51–74.

11. Eric Werner, *Mendelssohn: A New Image of the Composer and His Age*, trans. Dika Newlin (Westport, Conn.: Greenwood, 1963), 149. In *The Harmonicon* review (London, vol. 7 [August, 1829]: 204), Sontag is listed as the organizer of the concert, not Mendelssohn.

12. Letter of 10 April 1833, in Karl Klingemann [jr.], *Felix Mendelssohn Bartholdys Briefwechsel mit Legationsrat Karl Klingemann* (Essen: G. D. Baedeker, 1909), 114–15. A number of conductor's annotations are written in English on the score. Moreover, correspondence between Klingemann and Mendelssohn refers to the composer's difficulties with the revision of the concerto in anticipation of a performance with Moscheles in London. Describing his efforts at revision to Klingemann, Mendelssohn complained "mit dem geht es gar nicht, jeder Gedanke klopft erst zwanzig Mal an die Tür ehe er hereinkommt, und sehr oft wird geklopft, aber es kommt kein Gedanke herein" (it doesn't go very well, every idea knocks first twenty times on the door before it comes in, and often there are many knocks, but no idea comes in). My translation.

13. Karl-Heinz Köhler, ed., *F. Mendelssohn: Konzert für zwei Klaviere und Orchester E-dur*, Leipziger Ausgabe der Werke Felix Mendelssohn Bartholdys, Serie II, Bd. 4. (Leipzig: Deutsche Verlag für Musik, 1960; 2nd printing, 1971).

14. As noted on the title page of Moscheles's copy of Mendelssohn's concerto, D-B Mendelssohn Archiv, Mus. ms. 14325/4. This point will be discussed later in this essay.

15. See Edwin J. Simon, "The Double Exposition in Classic Concerto Form" (Ph.D. diss., University of California, Berkeley, 1954). See also Edwin J. Simon, "Double Exposition in the

xiii

Classic Concerto," *Journal of the American Musicological Society* 10 (1957): 111–18.

16. *NG* "Mendelssohn," 136.

17. This seven-part schema stems from Daniel N. Leeson and Robert D. Levin, "On the Authenticity of K. Anh. C 14.01 (297b), a *Symphonia concertante* for Winds and Orchestra," *Mozart-Jahrbuch* 1976/77 (Kassel: Bärenreiter, 1978), 73.

18. Sir Donald Francis Tovey, *Essays in Musical Analysis*, vol. 3, *Concertos* (London: Oxford University Press, 1936), 3.

19. W. A. Mozart, *Neue Ausgabe sämtlicher Werke: Konzerte für ein oder mehrere Klaviere und Orchester mit Kadenzen*, Serie V, Werkgruppe 15: Band 7, ed. Herman Beck (Kassel: Bärenreiter, 1959, ed. No. BA 4519); also, Joseph Kerman, ed., *Mozart: Piano Concerto in C Major, K. 503*, Norton Critical Score (New York and London: W. W. Norton, 1970).

20. Jan LaRue, *Guidelines for Style Analysis* (New York: W. W. Norton, 1970; rev. ed., Warren, Mich.: Harmonie Park Press, 1992).

21. The time lines contain three columns, which are read down the page in the following order: *Ritornello 1* (or *Tutti Exposition*), *Solo Exposition* (with the *Development* section at the end of this second column), and *Recapitulation*. Douglas Johnson created the prototype for these time lines. I am grateful to him for allowing me to appropriate his model, and for his assistance with the construction of the time lines used in this essay. Any errors within the time lines are my own. For more on changes to piano concerto form in the early nineteenth century, see Stephan D. Lindeman, *Structural Novelty and Tradition in the Early Romantic Piano Concerto* (Stuyvesant, N.Y.: Pendragon Press, 1999).

22. Although only six of Mozart's twenty-three original piano concertos were published in his lifetime, all had been published by 1806 (Ludwig von Köchel, *Chronologisch-thematisches Verzeichnis sämtlicher Tonwerke Wolfgang Amade Mozarts* [Leipzig, 1862]; 6th rev. ed. by F. Giegling, A. Weinmann, and G. Sievers [Wiesbaden: Breitkopf & Härtel, 1964]). The Mozart piano concertos were apparently quite popular in the first half of the nineteenth century, ranking third in a list of twenty in frequency of performance (behind Beethoven and Moscheles) in the number of performances at the London Philharmonic Society concerts through 1850 and seventh in a list of eighteen (following Hummel, Weber, Mendelssohn, Beethoven, Cramer, and Moscheles) of the most frequently performed piano concertos in London from 1801 to 1850. For more information, see Therese M. Ellsworth, "The Piano Concerto in London Concert Life Between 1801 and 1850" (Ph.D. diss., University of Cincinnati, 1991), 103, 231.

23. Felix Mendelssohn, Piano Concerto in A Minor, holograph. D-B, Mus. ms. autogr. F. Mendelssohn 3, 29–84. As of this writing, the concerto has not been published as part of the *Leipziger Ausgabe der Werke Felix Mendelssohn Bartholdys*. At least one recording of the work is available, as performed by Cyprien Katsaris with the Franz Liszt Chamber Orchestra, János Rolla, Leader, originally released by Teldec Records in 1984, re-released by the Musical Heritage Society, compact disc number MHS 512251W (1988). For a detailed discussion of the circumstances surrounding the compositional process in the A minor concerto see Marian Wilson, "Felix Mendelssohn's Works for Solo Piano and Orchestra: Sources and Composition" (Ph.D. diss., Florida State University, 1993), 8–46. She points out the apparent influence of Hummel on young Mendelssohn's work, particularly the similarity of primary themes between Mendelssohn's first movement and that of the Hummel A minor concerto, op. 85. Hummel had been a guest at the Mendelssohn family home in Berlin in the spring of 1821, and Mendelssohn later renewed contact with the elder composer during his visit with Goethe in Weimar in September of that year. In Wilson's formal analysis of the first movement (p. 14), she indicates that the soloist enters in measure 56. According to my counting, however, the soloist does not enter until measure 71. She also delineates each of the first movements analyzed in her dissertation according to the dictates of sonata, rather than concerto form. Therefore, she does not use such terms as *Ritornello 1, Solo Exposition*, etc. Following this procedure, her demarcation of the development section begins at the close of the (solo) exposition, whereas concerto form would see this as the beginning of the second ritornello; the development proper would generally commence with the soloist's reentry after the second ritornello.

24. Elise Polko, *Erinnerungen an Felix Mendelssohn-Bartholdy* (Leipzig, 1868); trans. Lady [Grace] Wallace under the title *Reminiscences of Mendelssohn-Bartholdy* (New York: Leypoldt & Holt; repr. Macomb, Ill.: Glenbridge Publishing, 1987), 3–7.

25. Further evidence that this key relationship was very much on the mind of the young composer is found in the violin concerto from the previous year (1822), also in D minor (Felix Mendelssohn, Concerto for Violin in D Minor, holograph. D-B, Mus. ms. autogr. F. Mendelssohn 3, 85–118); this concerto is one of three of the five early concertos printed in the Leipziger Ausgabe (Serie II, Bd. 6, ed. Renata Unger, 1973). In the development section of the first movement (m. 227 ff.) a deceptive resolution from F major to a brief passage in D♭ major also occurs. For more on this piece, see Todd's discussion in "The Instrumental Music of Felix Mendelssohn-Bartholdy" (Ph.D. diss., Yale University, 1979), 2:353. At least two recordings are available: Gidon Kremer and Martha Argerich with the Orpheus Chamber Orchestra, Deutsche Grammophon compact disk number D 105583 (released in 1989); and Thomas Zehetmair, violin, with the Franz Liszt Chamber Orchestra, János Rolla, Leader, originally released by Teldec Records in 1984, re-released by the Musical Heritage Society, compact disc number MHS 512251W (1988).

26. See Lindeman, "Mendelssohn and Moscheles," which examines Mendelssohn's revisions of the E major concerto in greater detail.

27. The E major concerto has not been very well received by modern critics; see, for example, Werner's criticism in "Two Unpublished Concertos," 130–38; Werner, *Mendelssohn*, 55–57; and Todd, "The Instrumental Music," 2:356–57.

28. Mendelssohn's letter to his father of 10 July 1829 is reprinted in *Mendelssohn Letters*, ed. Elvers, 74–78; the composer's letter to his Uncle Nathan is quoted in Werner, "Two Unpublished Concertos," 131; Klingemann's two reports are also cited in Werner, "Two Unpublished Concertos," 130; the *Berliner allgemeine musikalische Zeitung* article is in vol. 6 (1829): 279 ff. (also cited in Werner, "Two Unpublished Concertos," p. 130); *The Harmonicon* notice is cited in note 11; Moscheles's reference is found in *Moscheles's Leben*, 151.

29. *Mendelssohn Letters*, ed. Elvers, 74–75.

30. Leonard Milton Phillips, Jr., "The Leipzig Conservatory: 1843–1881" (Ph.D. diss., Indiana University, 1979), 262, 263. Natalie Schilling, from Leipzig, student no. 644, enrolled in 1857; Bertha Seraphine Schwalbe, from Lichtenstein, student no. 721, enrolled in 1858.

31. Title page of D-B Mendelssohn Archiv, Mus. ms. 14325/4.

32. "Es war interessant zu hören wie der 14 jährige Mendelssohn alla Mozart komponiert hatte. Im Buche der Programme hatte ich es eingeschrieben als von F. Knospe." My translation. I am grateful to Dr. Ingeborg Heussner for kindly supplying me with this information from her notes, including the quotation from Moscheles's diary (not contained within Charlotte Moscheles's *Aus Moscheles's Leben* edition of the diaries). The quote is found in a catalogue published in 1911 by the Berlin antiquarian dealer Leo Liepmannssohn, advertising the sale of Moscheles's copy of the concerto. Liepmannsohn noted that Moscheles's son Felix had furnished the dealer with this quote from his father's diary. For more on Moscheles, see Heussner's dissertation, *Ignaz Moscheles in seinen Klavier-Sonaten, Kammermusikwerken, und -Konzerten* (University of Marburg, 1963).

Plate 1. Felix Mendelssohn, Concerto for Two Pianos and Orchestra in E Major. Staatsbibliothek zu Berlin Preußischer Kulturbesitz, Musikabteilung mit Mendelssohn Archiv, Mendelssohn Nachlaß, Mus. ms. MN 15, p. 1.

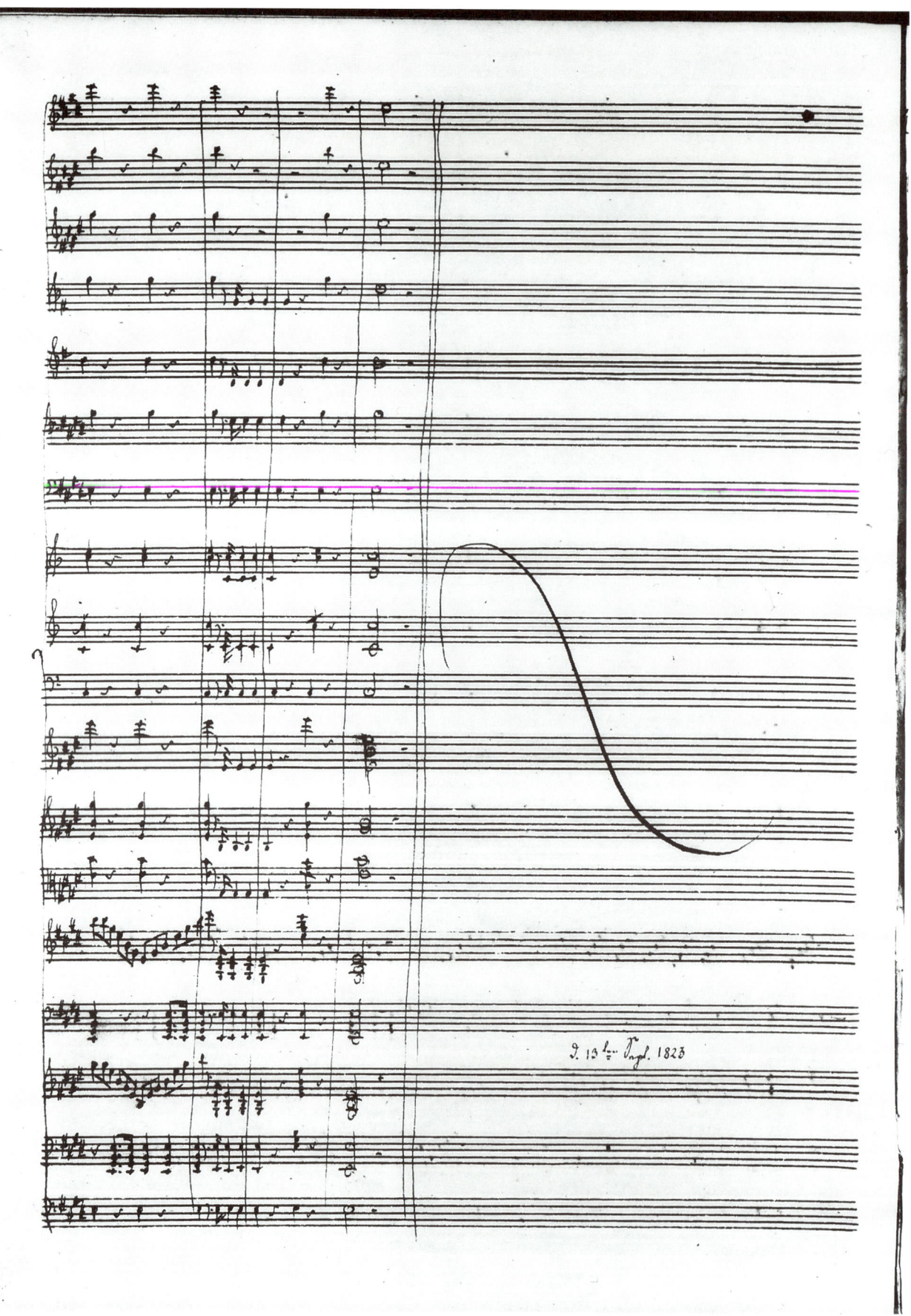

Plate 2. Felix Mendelssohn, Concerto for Two Pianos and Orchestra in E Major. Staatsbibliothek zu Berlin Preußischer Kulturbesitz, Musikabteilung mit Mendelssohn Archiv, Mendelssohn Nachlaß, Mus. ms. MN 15, p. 68.

Plate 3. Ignaz Moscheles, manuscript copy of Felix Mendelssohn's Concerto for Two Pianos and Orchestra in E Major. Staatsbibliothek zu Berlin Preußischer Kulturbesitz, Musikabteilung mit Mendelssohn Archiv, Mus. ms. 14325/4, p. 1.

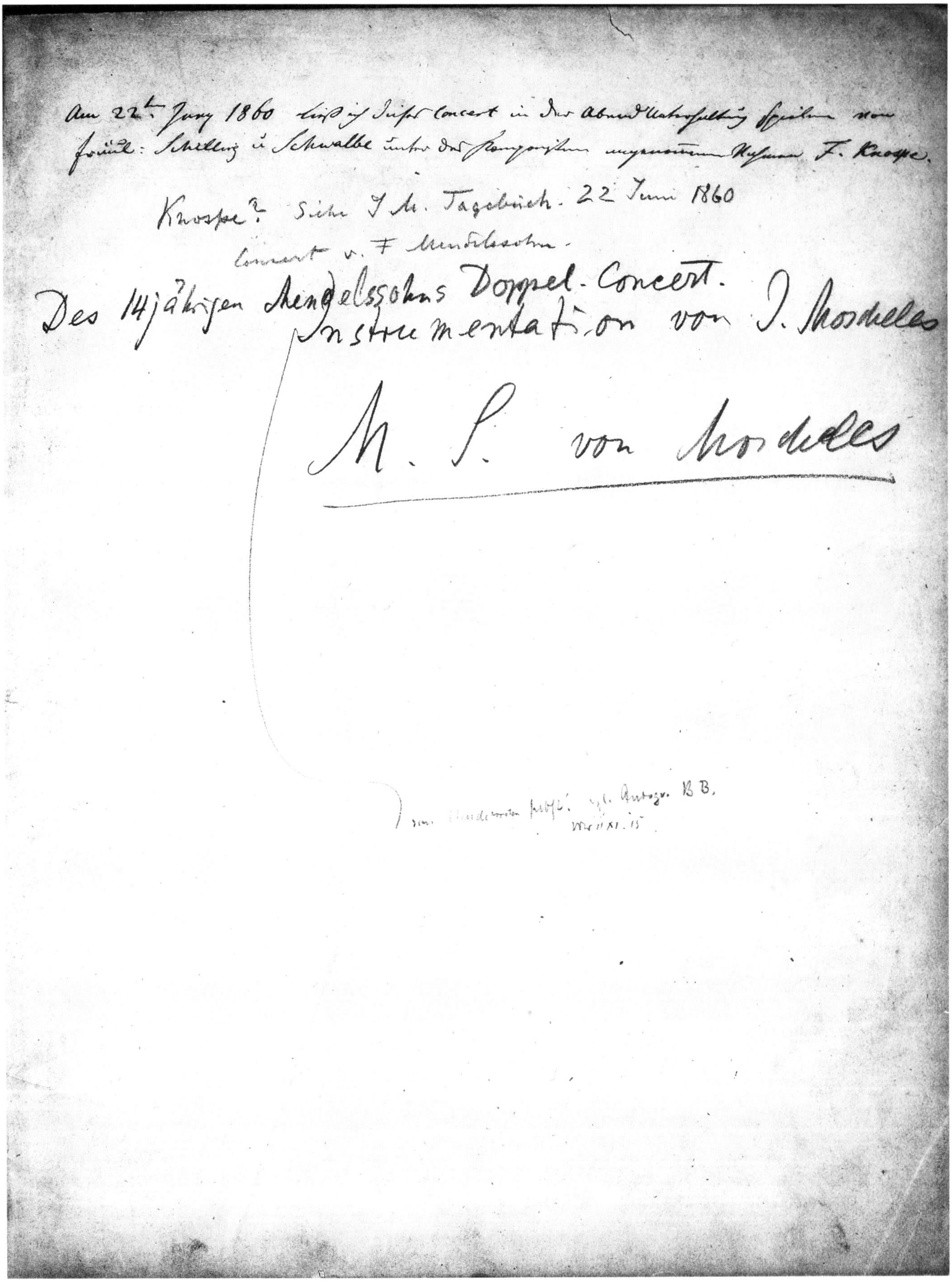

Plate 4. Ignaz Moscheles, manuscript copy of Felix Mendelssohn's Concerto for Two Pianos and Orchestra in E Major. Staatsbibliothek zu Berlin Preußischer Kulturbesitz, Musikabteilung mit Mendelssohn Archiv, Mus. ms. 14325/4, cover page.

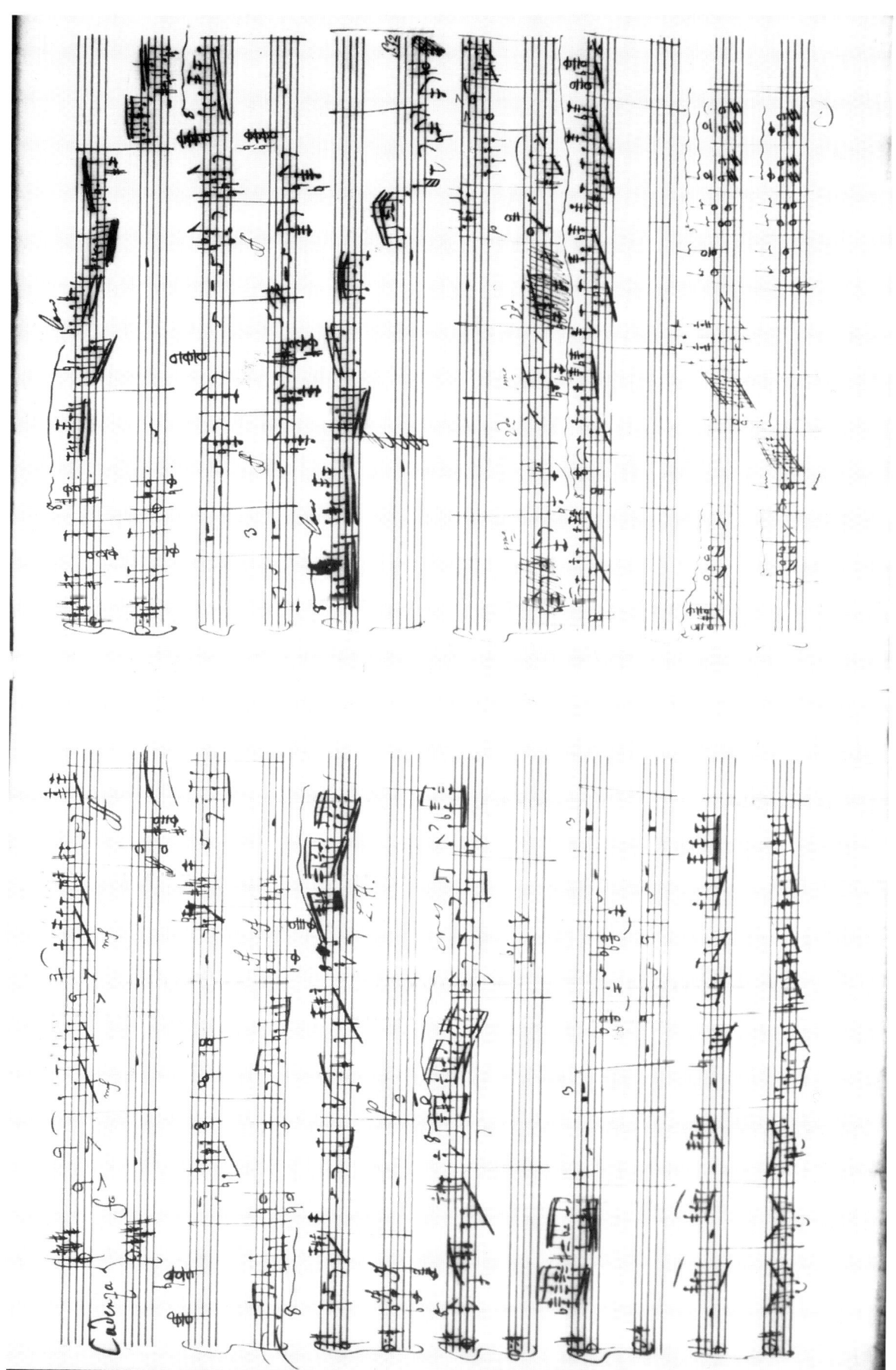

Plate 5. Ignaz Moscheles, piano 1 cadenza for the first movement of Felix Mendelssohn's Concerto for Two Pianos and Orchestra in E Major. Bodleian Library, Oxford University. Mendelssohn Papers, C. 86.

Plate 6. Felix Mendelssohn, Concerto for Two Pianos and Orchestra in E Major. Staatsbibliothek zu Berlin Preußischer Kulturbesitz, Musikabteilung mit Mendelssohn Archiv, Mendelssohn Nachlaß, Mus. ms. MN 15, p. 55.

Plate 7. Felix Mendelssohn, Concerto for Two Pianos and Orchestra in E Major. Staatsbibliothek zu Berlin Preußischer Kulturbesitz, Musikabteilung mit Mendelssohn Archiv, Mendelssohn Nachlaß, Mus. ms. MN 15, p. 66.

Plate 8. Felix Mendelssohn, Concerto for Two Pianos and Orchestra in E Major. Staatsbibliothek zu Berlin Preußischer Kulturbesitz, Musikabteilung mit Mendelssohn Archiv, Mendelssohn Nachlaß, Mus. ms. MN 15, p. 59, mm. 330/388–336/394.

Plate 9. Ignaz Moscheles, manuscript copy of Felix Mendelssohn's Concerto for Two Pianos and Orchestra in E Major. Staatsbibliothek zu Berlin Preußischer Kulturbesitz, Musikabteilung mit Mendelssohn Archiv, Mus. ms. 14325/4, pp. 38–39, mm. 328/386–336/394.

Plate 9. Continued.

Concerto for Two Pianos and Orchestra in E Major
Original Version of the First Movement

10

11

52
[55]
Fl.
Ob. 1
Ob. 2
Cl. 1
in A
Cl. 2
in A
Bn. 1
Bn. 2
Hn. 1, 2
in E
Tpt. 1, 2
in E
Timp.
in E/B
Pn. 1
Pn. 2
Vn. 1
Vn. 2
div.
Va.
pizz.
arco
pizz.
Vc.
pizz.
Cb.

57
[60]
Fl.
Ob. 1
Ob. 2
Cl. 1 in A
Cl. 2 in A
Bn. 1
Bn. 2
Hn. 1, 2 in E
Tpt. 1, 2 in E
Timp. in E/B
Pn. 1
Pn. 2
Vn. 1
Vn. 2
Va.
Vc. Cb.
p
(cresc.)
Ob.
Bn.
cresc.
(p)
(al)
arco

62
Fl.
Ob. 1
Ob. 2
Cl. 1
in A
Cl. 2
in A
Bn. 1
Bn. 2
Hn. 1, 2
in E
Tpt. 1, 2
in E
Timp.
in E/B
Pn. 1
Pn. 2
Vn. 1
Vn. 2
unis.
Va.
Vc.
Cb.

65
[65]
Fl.
Ob. 1
Ob. 2
Cl. 1 in A
Cl. 2 in A
Bn. 1
Bn. 2
Hn. 1, 2 in F
Tpt. 1, 2 in E
Timp. in E/B
Pn. 1
Pn. 2
ff
Vn. 1
Vn. 2
Va.
Vc. Cb.

68
[70]
Fl.
Ob. 1
Ob. 2
Cl. 1 in A
Cl. 2 in A
Bn. 1
Bn. 2
Hn. 1, 2 in E
Tpt. 1, 2 in E
Timp. in E/B
Pn. 1
Pn. 2
Vn. 1
Vn. 2
Va.
Vc. Cb.
ff
p
solo
[a 2]
Cl.

17

18

19

88
[90]
Fl.
Ob. 1
Cl. 1
Bn. 1
Bn. 2
Hn.
1, 2
Pn. 1
solo
ff
(sf)
Pn. 2
Vn. 1
Vn. 2
Va.
Vc.
Cb.
91
[9]
Pn. 1
Pn. 2
ff

21

100
[100]
Fl.
Ob. 1
Ob. 2
Cl. 1
in A
Cl. 2
in A
Bn. 1
Bn. 2
Hn. 1, 2
in E
Tpt. 1, 2
in E
Timp.
in E/B
Pn. 1
Pn. 2
Vn. 1
Vn. 2
Va.
Vc.
Cb.
8va
f
p

[FMB cut: skip 6 m.]
103
Fl.
Ob. 1
Ob. 2
Cl. 1 in A
Cl. 2 in A
Bn. 1
Bn. 2
Hn. 1, 2 in E
Tpt. 1, 2 in E
Timp. in E/B
Pn. 1
p
3
Pn. 2
fp
Vn. 1
Vn. 2
Va.
Vc. Cb.

107
[103]
Fl.
Ob. 1
Ob. 2
Cl. 1 in A
Cl. 2 in A
Bn. 1
Bn. 2
Hn. 1, 2 in E
Tpt. 1, 2 in E
Timp. in E/B
Pn. 1
Tutti
Pn. 2
Tutti
Vn. 1
Vn. 2
Va.
Vc. Cb.

C
110 [104]
[105]
Fl.
Ob. 1
Ob. 2
Cl. 1 in A
Cl. 2 in A
Bn. 1
Bn. 2
Hn. 1, 2 in E
Tpt. 1, 2 in E
Timp. in E/B
Pn. 1
f
Pn. 2
Vn. 1
Vn. 2
Va.
Vc. Cb.

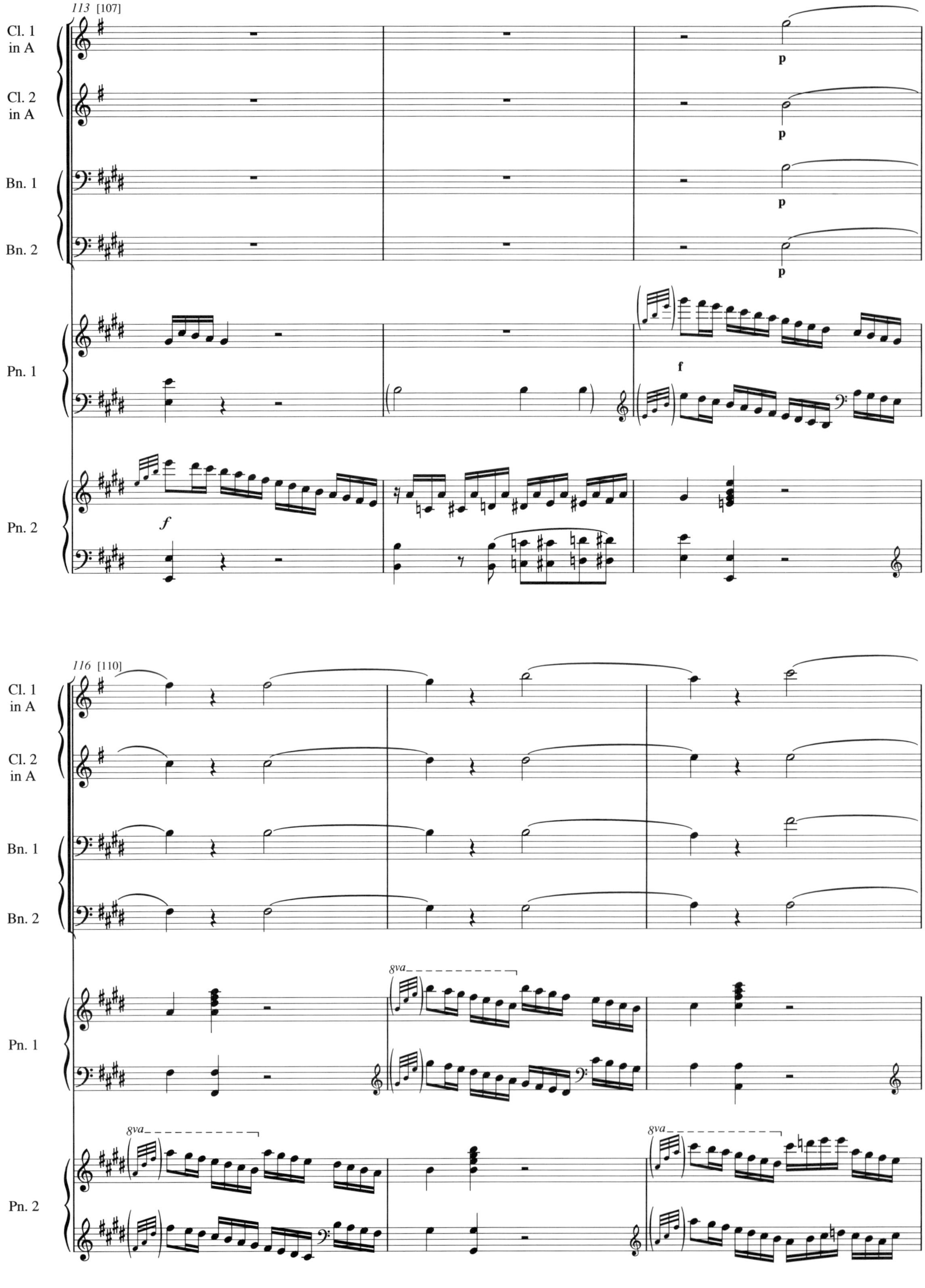
113 [107]
Cl. 1 in A
Cl. 2 in A
Bn. 1
Bn. 2
Pn. 1
Pn. 2
p
f
116 [110]
8va

27

122 [116]
Fl.
Ob. 1
Ob. 2
Cl. 1 in A
Cl. 2 in A
Bn. 1
Bn. 2
Hn. 1, 2 in E
Tpt. 1, 2 in E
Timp. in E/B
Pn. 1
Pn. 2
Vn. 1
Vn. 2
Va.
Vc. Cb.
f
p
tr
(cresc.)
(al)
(f)
8va

29

130 [124]
[125]
Bn. 1
Bn. 2
Pn. 1
(dolce)
Pn. 2
Vn. 1
Vn. 2
Va.
Vc.
Cb.
135 [129]
[130]
Hn. 1, 2
in E
p
Pn. 1
tr
(p)
Pn. 2
pizz.
Vc.
Cb.
p

31

32

149 [143]
[145]
Cl. 1 in A
Cl. 2 in A
Bn. 1
Bn. 2
Hn. 1, 2 in E
Pn. 1
Pn. 2
Vn. 1
Vn. 2
Va.
Vc. Cb.
p

153 [147]
[150]
Cl. 1 in A
Cl. 2 in A
Bn. 1
Bn. 2
Hn. 1, 2 in E
a 2
1
Pn. 1
Pn. 2
Vn. 1
Vn. 2
Va.
div.
[unis.]
div.
Vc. Cb.

157 [151]
[un poco ritard.]
Cl. 1 in A
Cl. 2 in A
Bn. 1
Bn. 2
Hn. 1, 2 in E
Pn. 1
(dim.)
Pn. 2
dim.
[un poco ritard.]
Vn. 1
Vn. 2
[unis.]
Va.
Vc. Cb.

E [a tempo]
161 [155]
Fl.
Ob. 1
Ob. 2
Cl. 1 in A
Cl. 2 in A
Bn. 1
Bn. 2
Hn. 1, 2 in E
Tpt. 1, 2 in E
Timp. in E/B
Pn. 1
Pn. 2
[a tempo]
Vn. 1
Vn. 2
Va.
Vc. Cb.

164 [158]
[160]
solo
Fl.
Ob. 1
Ob. 2
Cl. 1 in A
Cl. 2 in A
Bn. 1
Bn. 2
Hn. 1, 2 in E
Tpt. 1, 2 in E
Timp. in E/B
Pn. 1
Pn. 2
8va
Vn. 1
Vn. 2
Va.
Vc. Cb.

38

170 [164]
[165]
Pn. 1
Pn. 2
Vn. 1
Vn. 2
Va.
Vc.
Cb.
173
[FMB cut: skip 11 m.]
8va
loco
p
pizz.
div.

40

179
Fl.
Ob. 1
Ob. 2
Cl. 1 in A
Cl. 2 in A
Bn. 1
Bn. 2
Hn. 1, 2 in E
Tpt. 1, 2 in E
Timp. in E/B
Pn. 1
Ob.
Cl.
Bn.
Pn. 2
Vn. 1
arco
Vn. 2
arco
[unis.]
Va.
Vc. Cb.
arco

42

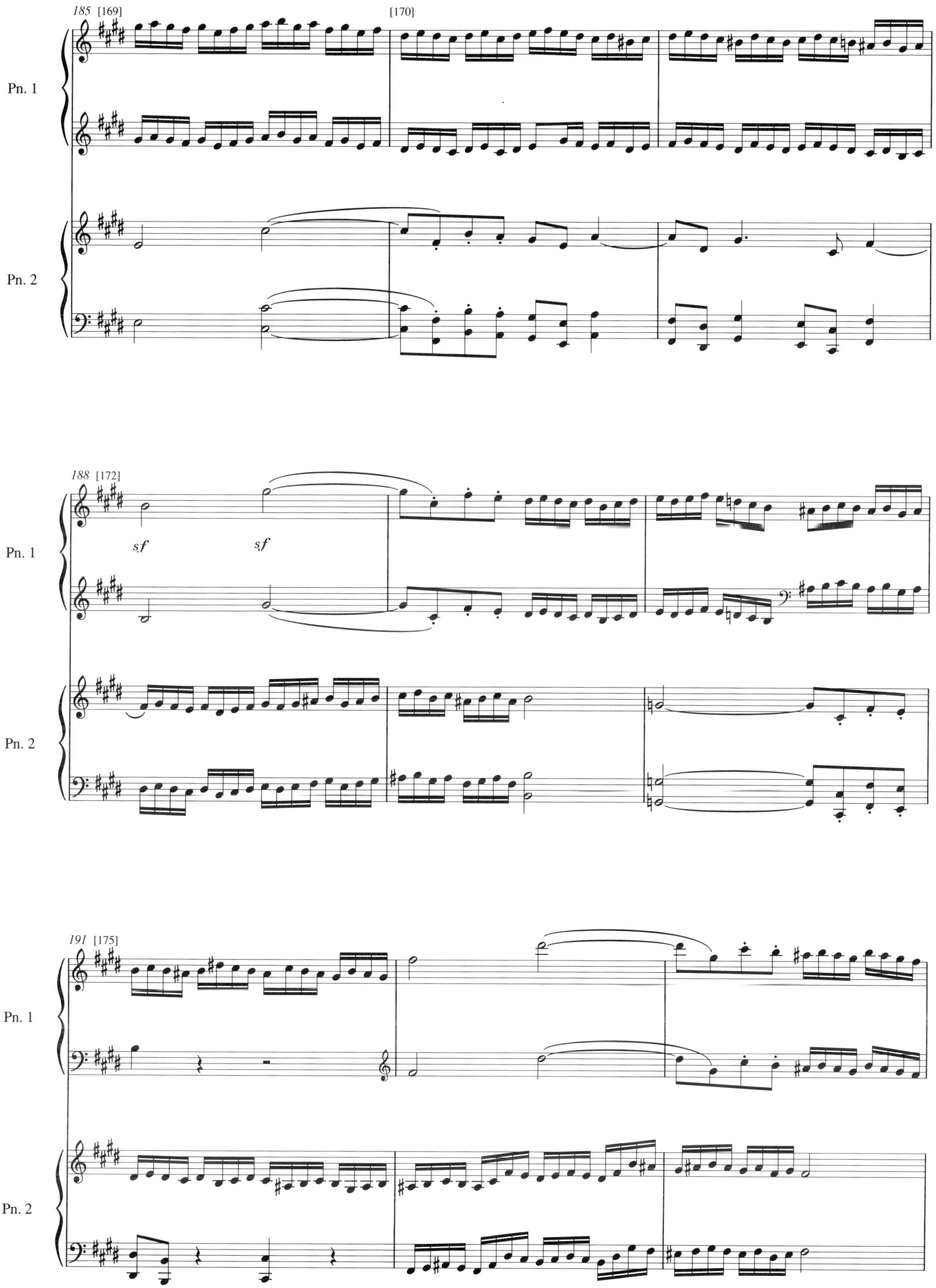
185 [169]
[170]
Pn. 1
Pn. 2
188 [172]
sf
sf
Pn. 1
Pn. 2
191 [175]
Pn. 1
Pn. 2

194 [178]
[180]
Pn. 1
(dim.)
(sfz)
Pn. 2
Vc.
Cb.
pizz.
197 [181]
Hn. 1, 2
in E
1
p
Pn. 1
(cresc.)
f
Pn. 2
(cresc.)
f
Vn. 1
pizz.
(cresc.)
Vn. 2
pizz.
(cresc.)
Va.
pizz.
(cresc.)
Vc.
Cb.
(cresc.)

45

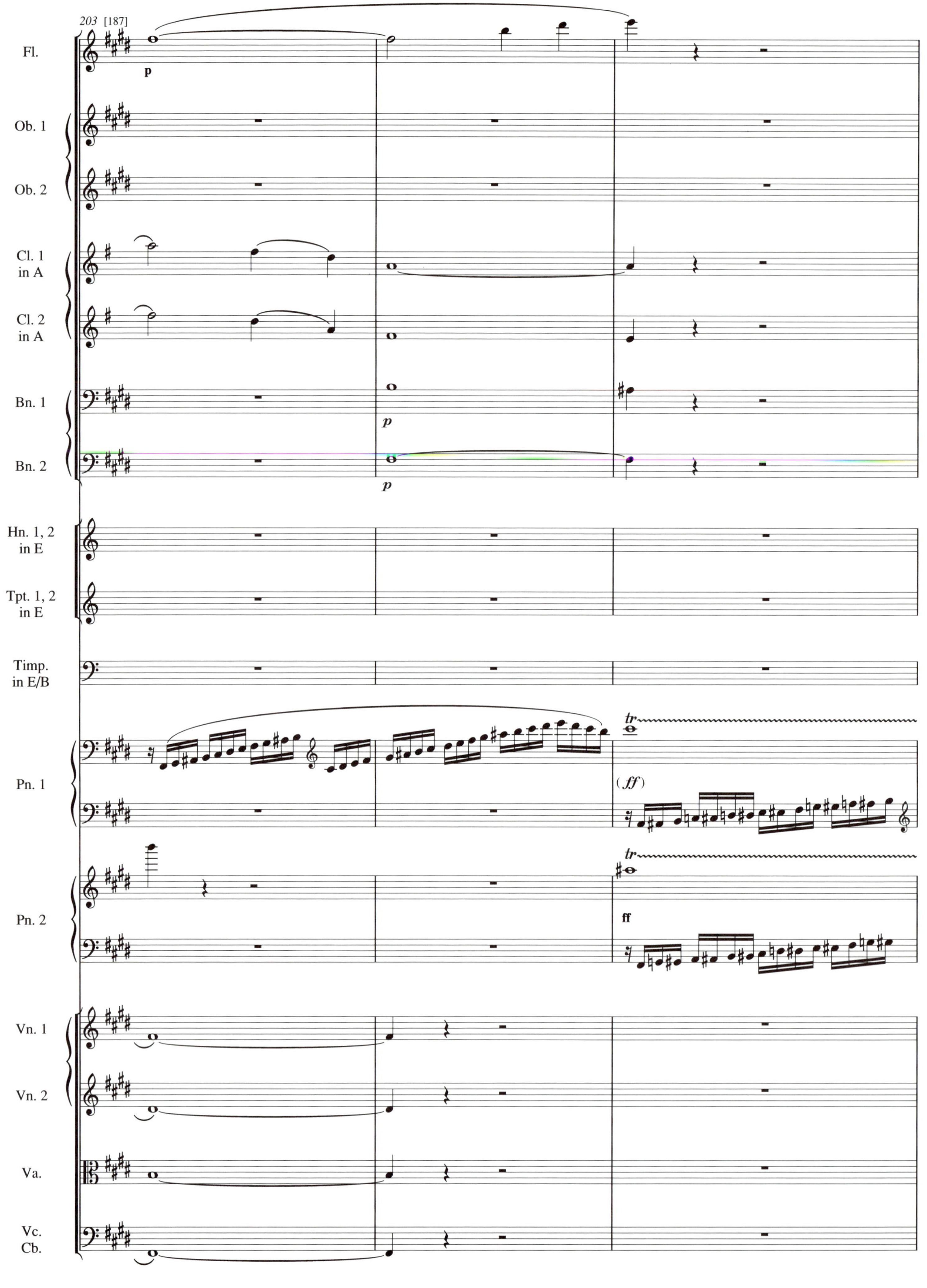
203 [187]
Fl.
Ob. 1
Ob. 2
Cl. 1 in A
Cl. 2 in A
Bn. 1
Bn. 2
Hn. 1, 2 in E
Tpt. 1, 2 in E
Timp. in E/B
Pn. 1
Pn. 2
Vn. 1
Vn. 2
Va.
Vc. Cb.

47

211 [195]
Fl.
Ob. 1
Ob. 2
Cl. 1 in A
Cl. 2 in A
Bn. 1
Bn. 2
Hn. 1, 2 in E
[a 2]
Tpt. 1, 2 in E
[a 2]
(f)
Timp. in E/B
Tutti Vn.
Pn. 1
Tutti
Pn. 2
f
Vn. 1
Vn. 2
Va.
Vc. Cb.
f

49

217 [201]
Fl.
Ob. 1
Ob. 2
Cl. 1 in A
Cl. 2 in A
Bn. 1
Bn. 2
Hn. 1, 2 in E
a 2
Tpt. 1, 2 in E
[a 2]
Timp. in E/B
Pn. 1
Pn. 2
Vn. 1
Vn. 2
Va.
Vc. Cb.
ff

51

52

53

54

55

239 [207]
Fl.
Ob. 1
Ob. 2
Cl. 1 in A
Cl. 2 in A
Bn. 1
Bn. 2
Hn. 1, 2 in E
Tpt. 1, 2 in E
Timp. in E/B
Pn. 1
(ad lib.)
fp
fp
Pn. 2
Vn. 1
Vn. 2
Va.
Vc. Cb.
(f)

57

58

59

H
257 [225]
Fl.
Ob. 1
Ob. 2
Cl. 1 in A
Cl. 2 in A
Bn. 1
Bn. 2
Hn. 1, 2 in E
Tpt. 1, 2 in E
Timp.
Pn. 1
Pn. 2
Hn.
Vn. 1
Vn. 2
Va.
Vc. Cb.

260 [228]
[230]
Fl.
Ob. 1
Ob. 2
Cl. 1 in A
Cl. 2 in A
Bn. 1
Bn. 2
Hn. 1, 2 in E
Tpt. 1, 2 in E
Timp.
Pn. 1
Pn. 2
Vn. 1
Vn. 2
Va.
Vc. Cb.

263 [231]
Fl.
Ob. 1
Ob. 2
Cl. 1 in A
Cl. 2 in A
Bn. 1
Bn. 2
Hn. 1, 2 in E
Tpt. 1, 2 in E
Timp.
Pn. 1
Pn. 2
Vn. 1
Vn. 2
Va.
Vc. Cb.
p
mf
f
pizz.
arco

266 [234]
[235]
Fl.
Ob. 1
Ob. 2
Cl. 1 in A
Cl. 2 in A
Bn. 1
Bn. 2
Hn. 1, 2 in E
Tpt. 1, 2 in E
Timp.
Pn. 1
Pn. 2
Vn. 1
Vn. 2
Va.
Vc. Cb.
a 2
p
f
mf

269 [237]
Fl.
Ob. 1
Ob. 2
Cl. 1 in A
Cl. 2 in A
Bn. 1
Bn. 2
Hn. 1, 2 in E
Tpt. 1, 2 in E
Timp.
Pn. 1
Pn. 2
Vn. 1
Vn. 2
Va.
Vc. Cb.
p
mf
pizz.

272 [240]
Fl.
Ob. 1
Ob. 2
Cl. 1 in A
Cl. 2 in A
Bn. 1
Bn. 2
Hn. 1, 2 in E
Tpt. 1, 2 in E
Timp.
Pn. 1
Str.
8va
Pn. 2
Vn. 1
Vn. 2
Va.
p
Vc. Cb.

275 [243]
Fl.
Ob. 1
Ob. 2
Cl. 1
in A
Cl. 2
in A
Bn. 1
Bn. 2
Hn. 1, 2
in E
Tpt. 1, 2
in E
Timp.
Pn. 1
Pn. 2
Vn. 1
Vn. 2
Va.
Vc.
Cb.
p
8va
loco
Vn.
Cl.
Bn.

67

281 [249]
Pn. 1
sf
sf
Pn. 2
sf
sf
Vn. 1
Vn. 2
Va.
Vc.
Cb.
284 [252]
J
Pn. 1
Pn. 2
sf
Vn. 1
p
Vn. 2
p
Va.
p
Vc.
Cb.
p

287 [FMB cut: skip 29 m.]
Fl.
Cl. 1 in A
solo
p
solo
Pn. 1
tr
Pn. 2
f
Basso
Vn. 1
Vn. 2
Va.
Vc. Cb.
290
Pn. 1
tr
ff
Pn. 2
Vn. 1
Vn. 2
p
Va.
Vc. Cb.

292a
292b
292c
Vi-
-de
Fl.
Ob. 1
Ob. 2
Cl. 1 in A
Cl. 2 in A
Bn. 1
Bn. 2
Hn. 1, 2 in E
Tpt. 1, 2 in E
Timp.
Pn. 1
Tutti
Pn. 2
Tutti
Vn. 1
Vn. 2
Va.
Vc. Cb.

71

297
Fl.
Ob. 1
Ob. 2
Cl. 1
Cl. 2
Bn. 1
Bn. 2
Hn. 1, 2
Tpt. 1, 2
Timp.
Pn. 1
Pn. 2
Vn. 1
Vn. 2
Va.
Vc.
Cb.
solo
solo
Bn.

301
Fl.
Ob. 1
Ob. 2
Cl. 1
Cl. 2
Bn. 1
Bn. 2
Hn. 1, 2
Tpt. 1, 2
Timp.
Pn. 1
Pn. 2
Vn. 1
Vn. 2
Va.
Vc.
Cb.

304
Fl.
Ob. 1
Ob. 2
Cl. 1
Cl. 2
Bn. 1
Bn. 2
Hn. 1, 2
Tpt. 1, 2
Timp.
Pn. 1
Pn. 2
Vn. 1
Vn. 2
Va.
Vc.
Cb.
f
sf
p
fp

307
Fl.
Ob. 1
Ob. 2
Cl. 1
Cl. 2
Bn. 1
Bn. 2
Hn. 1, 2
Tpt. 1, 2
Timp.
Pn. 1
Pn. 2
Vn. 1
Vn. 2
Va.
Vc.
Cb.
solo
[Cl.] Bn.
Bn.
cresc.
cresc.

310
Fl.
Ob. 1
Ob. 2
Cl. 1
Cl. 2
Bn. 1
Bn. 2
Hn. 1, 2
Tpt. 1, 2
Timp.
Pn. 1
Cl.
Pn. 2
Basso
Vn. 1
Vn. 2
Va.
Vc.
Cb.

313 [255]
Fl.
Ob. 1
Ob. 2
Cl. 1 in A
Cl. 2 in A
Bn. 1
Bn. 2
Hn. 1, 2 in E
Tpt. 1, 2 in E
Timp.
Pn. 1
Pn. 2
Vn. 1
Vn. 2
Va.
Vc. Cb.
(pizz.)
(pizz.)
(pizz.)
(pizz.)

78

79

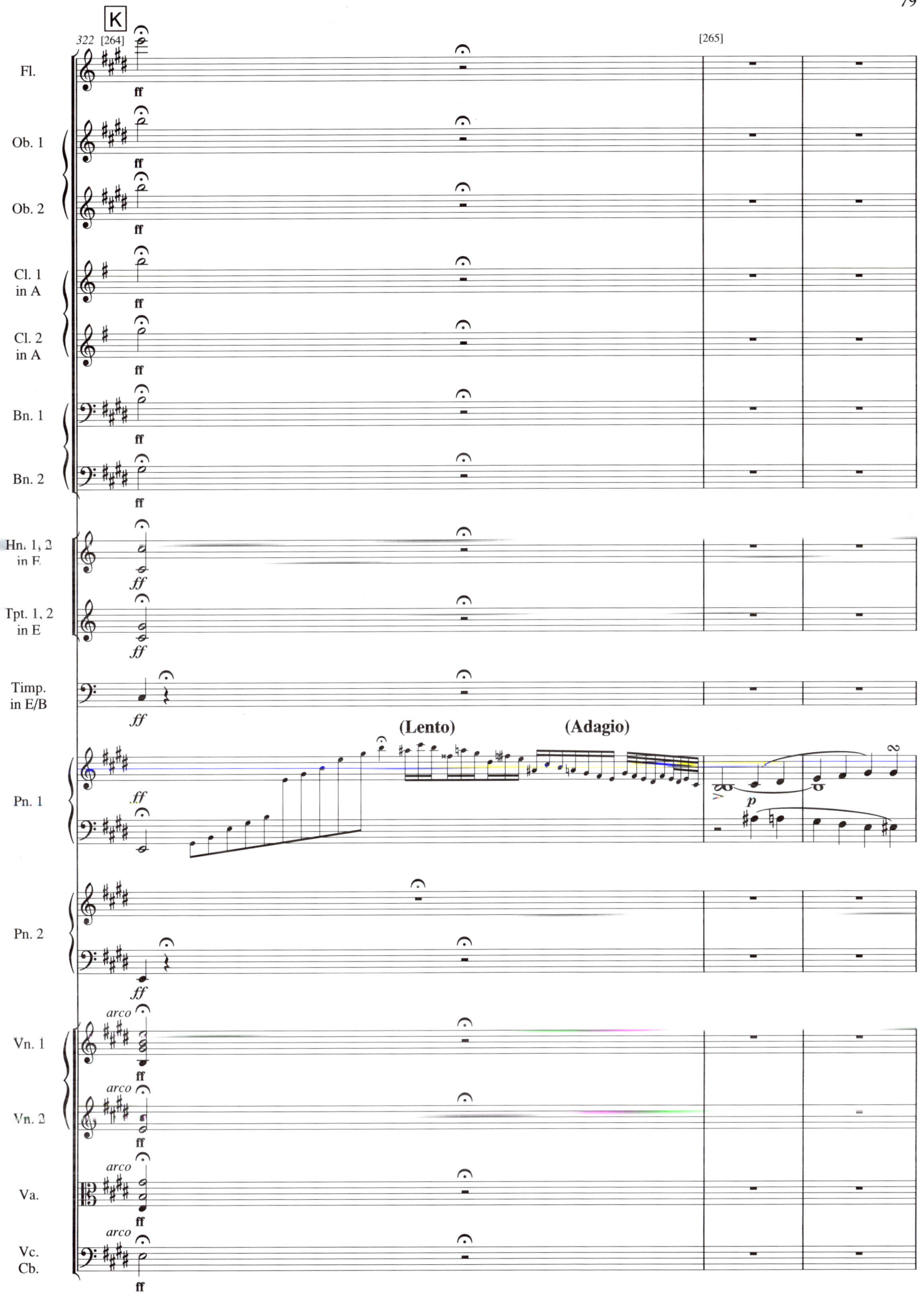

80

81

82

342 [284]
[285]
Fl.
Ob. 1
Ob. 2
Cl. 1 in A
Cl. 2 in A
Bn. 1
Bn. 2
Hn. 1, 2 in E
Tpt. 1, 2 in E
Timp. in E/B
Pn. 1
Pn. 2
Vn. 1
Vn. 2
Va.
Vc. Cb.
ff
sf
[>]
[>]

345 [287]
Fl.
Ob. 1
Ob. 2
Cl. 1 in A
Cl. 2 in A
Bn. 1
Bn. 2
[a 2]
Hn. 1, 2 in E
Tpt. 1, 2 in E
Timp. in E/B
Pn. 1
Pn. 2
Vn. 1
Vn. 2
Va.
Vc. Cb.

348 [290]
Fl.
Ob. 1
Ob. 2
Cl. 1 in A
Cl. 2 in A
Bn. 1
Bn. 2
solo
solo
Hn. 1, 2 in E
Tpt. 1, 2 in E
Timp. in E/B
Vn.
Bn.
Pn. 1
Pn. 2
Vn. 1
Vn. 2
Va.
Vc.
Cb.

353 [295]
Pn. 1
Pn. 2
Vn. 1
Vn. 2
Va.
Vc.
Cb.
357 [299]
[300]
Pn. 1
Pn. 2
Vn. 1
Vn. 2
Va.
Vc.
Cb.
p

361 [303]
[305]
Fl.
Ob. 1
Ob. 2
Cl. 1
in A
Cl. 2
in A
Bn. 1
Bn. 2
Hn. 1, 2
in E
p
Tpt. 1, 2
in E
Timp.
in E/B
Pn. 1
Pn. 2
Ped.
Vn. 1
Vn. 2
Va.
p
Vc.
Cb.

365 [307]
[310]
solo
Fl.
Ob. 1
Ob. 2
Cl. 1 in A
Cl. 2 in A
Bn. 1
Bn. 2
Hn. 1, 2 in E
Tpt. 1, 2 in E
Timp. in E/B
Pn. 1
Pn. 2
Vn. 1
Vn. 2
Va.
Vc. Cb.

89

373 [315]
Fl.
Ob. 1
Ob. 2
Cl. 1 in A
Cl. 2 in A
Bn. 1
Bn. 2
Hn. 1, 2 in E
soli
Tpt. 1, 2 in E
Timp. in E/B
Pn. 1
dolce
Pn. 2
[sf] p
Vn. 1
Vn. 2
[unis.]
Va.
Vc. Cb.

91

L
[a tempo]
381 [323]
[325]
Fl.
Ob. 1
Ob. 2
Cl. 1 in A
Cl. 2 in A
Bn. 1
Bn. 2
Hn. 1, 2 in E
Tpt. 1, 2 in E
Timp. in E/B
Pn. 1
Pn. 2
[a tempo]
Vn. 1
Vn. 2
Va.
Vc. Cb.

384 [326]
Fl.
Ob. 1
Ob. 2
Cl. 1 in A
Cl. 2 in A
Bn. 1
Bn. 2
Hn. 1, 2 in E
Tpt. 1, 2 in E
Timp. in E/B
Pn. 1
Pn. 2
Vn. 1
Vn. 2
Va.
Vc. Cb.
solo
f
p

94

95

393
[335]
Fl.
Ob. 1
Ob. 2
Cl. 1 in A
Cl. 2 in A
Bn. 1
Bn. 2
Hn. 1, 2 in E
Tpt. 1, 2 in E
Timp. in E/B
Pn. 1
Pn. 2
Vn. 1
Vn. 2
Va.
Vc. Cb.
f
ff
[simile]
fp
(pp)
(sf)
tr

397 [339]
[340]
Pn. 1
sf
(dim.)
Pn. 2
(dim.)
Vn. 1
tr
Vn. 2
tr
Va.
(pp)
(sf)
Vc.
Cb.
(pp)
401 [343]
[345]
Pn. 1
(p)
(cresc.)
Pn. 2
f
Vn. 1
Vn. 2
Va.
Vc.
Cb.

98

407 [349]
[350]
Fl.
p
Ob. 1
Ob. 2
Cl. 1 in A
p
Cl. 2 in A
p
Bn. 1
p
Bn. 2
p
Hn. 1, 2 in E
Tpt. 1, 2 in E
Timp. in E/B
Pn. 1
(ff)
dim.
Pn. 2
8va
Vn. 1
Vn. 2
Va.
Vc. Cb.

410 [352]
Pn. 1
f
dim.
p
dim.
Pn. 2
mf
dim.
Vn. 1
Vn. 2
Va.
Vc.
Cb.

413 [355]
solo
Fl.
(dolce)
Pn. 1
dolce
Pn. 2
p
(dim.)
Str.
Vn. 1
p
sf)
Vn. 2
p
Va.
p
Vc.
Cb.
p

416 [358]
[360]
Fl.
Ob. 1
Ob. 2
Cl. 1 in A
Cl. 2 in A
Bn. 1
Bn. 2
Hn. 1, 2 in E
Tpt. 1, 2 in E
Timp. in E/B
Pn. 1
Pn. 2
Vn. 1
Vn. 2
Va.
Vc. Cb.
solo
p
2 solo
Ob.
Bn.

419 [361]
Fl.
ff
(ff)
Ob. 1
(sf)
Ob. 2
Cl. 1 in A
sf
Cl. 2 in A
Bn. 1
Bn. 2
Hn. 1, 2 in E
2
Tpt. 1, 2 in E
Timp. in E/B
Fl.
Pn. 1
f
8va
Pn. 2
Vn. 1
pizz.
arco
Vn. 2
Va.
Vc. Cb.

M
422 [364]
[365]
Fl.
(sf) p
Ob. 1
(sfp)
Ob. 2
Cl. 1 in A
(sfp)
Cl. 2 in A
(p)
Bn. 1
Bn. 2
Hn. 1, 2 in E
a 2
(sf)
Tpt. 1, 2 in E
Timp. in E/B
pp
Pn. 1
(ff)
p
Pn. 2
Fl.
Vn.
(ff)
Vn. 1
p
Vn. 2
p
Va.
p
Vc. Cb.
p

104

428 [370]
Fl.
Ob. 1
Ob. 2
Cl. 1 in A
Cl. 2 in A
Bn. 1
Bn. 2
Hn. 1, 2 in E
a 2
Tpt. 1, 2 in E
Timp. in E/B
Pn. 1
Pn. 2
Vn. 1
Vn. 2
Va.
Vc. Cb.
(ff)
ff
f

106

107

108

*[small notes for M¹ cut]

109

443 [385]
Fl.
Ob. 1
Ob. 2
Cl. 1 in A
Cl. 2 in A
Bn. 1
Bn. 2
Hn. 1, 2 in E
Tpt. 1, 2 in E
Timp. in E/B
Pn. 1
Pn. 2
Vn. 1
Vn. 2
Va.
Vc. Cb.
ff

111

Critical Report

Sources

There is one primary source for Felix Mendelssohn's Concerto for Two Pianos and Orchestra in E major, and three supplementary manuscripts. They are described briefly here and discussed more fully in the editorial methods.

FMB

Felix Mendelssohn. Holograph score of the Concerto for Two Pianos and Orchestra in E major. Staatsbibliothek zu Berlin Preußischer Kulturbesitz, Musikabteilung mit Mendelssohn Archiv, Mendelssohn Nachlaß, Band 15 (see plate 1).

The first movement is sixty-eight pages in length and the last page of the movement is dated by the composer *d. 13ten Sept. 1823* (see plate 2).[1] The score is written on eighteen-stave paper, with the watermark *C & I Honig*. This manuscript is the sole extant autograph source for the work. Unlike many of Mendelssohn's other works, there are no surviving sketch materials for the concerto. The score was prepared with moderate care: in general, the manuscript is clearly legible, except for the passages where Mendelssohn has undertaken revisions, which will be discussed below. The upper right hand corner of the first page contains the inscription *L.e.g.G.*, Mendelssohn's invocation customarily encountered in first drafts, standing for "Lass es gelingen, Gott" (Let it succeed, O Lord) (see plate 1).[2]

M¹

Ignaz Moscheles. Holograph copy of Felix Mendelssohn's Concerto for Two Pianos and Orchestra in E major. Staatsbibliothek zu Berlin Preußischer Kulturbesitz, Musikabteilung mit Mendelssohn Archiv, Mus. ms. 14325/4 (see plate 3).

Moscheles scored the copy on 16-stave paper, with the pairs of winds and brass each reading from one staff, as opposed to the separate staves for the oboes, clarinets, and bassoons in Mendelssohn's autograph. Moscheles's copy carries no discernible watermark. The first movement is seventy-five pages in length. The manuscript is not dated, but contains the following four inscriptions, in four different hands (see plate 4), as identified by Karl-Heinz Köhler in the preface to his edition of the Concerto for Two Pianos and Orchestra in E major, revised version (Leipziger Ausgabe der Werke Felix Mendelssohn Bartholdys, Serie II, Bd. 4 [Leipzig, 1960]):

1. Moscheles's hand (in ink): "Am 22.ten Juni 1860 liess ich dieses Concert in der Abend Unterhaltung spielen von Fräul: Schilling u Schwalbe unter des Komponisten angenomenen Nahmen F. Knospe" (On 22 June 1860 I listened to this concerto in the evening concert played by Misses Schilling and Schwalbe, listed under the composer's name of F. Knospe).
2. Unidentified hand [a librarian's?] (in pencil): "Knospe? Siehe I. M. [Ignaz Moscheles] Tagebuch. 22 Juni 1860. Concert v. F. Mendelssohn" (Knospe? See I. M. diary, 22 June 1860. Concerto by F. Mendelssohn).[3]
3. Unidentified hand [another librarian's?] (in pencil): "Des 14 jahrigen Mendelssohns Doppel-Concert. Instrumentation von I. Moscheles. *M. S. Moscheles*" (The 14-year-old Mendelssohn's Double Concerto. Instrumentation by I. Moscheles).
4. Unidentified hand [another librarian's?] (in pencil): "von Mendelssohn selbst: vgl. Autogr. BB.WW ii XL. 15" (By Mendelssohn himself: compare the autograph BB. WW. ii XL. 15 [vol. 15 of the Mendelssohn Nachlaß]).

M²

Concert für 2 Pianoforte von M. F. A set of four string parts (*Violino I, Violino II, Viola, Violoncello e Basso*) in a copyist's hand created from, and catalogued with, M¹. Staatsbibliothek zu Berlin Preußischer Kulturbesitz, Musikabteilung mit Mendelssohn Archiv, Mus. ms 14325/4, 2–5. Forty-eight pages (all three movements).

M³

Ignaz Moscheles. Cadenza for the first movement of Felix Mendelssohn, Concerto for Two Pianos and Orchestra in E major, for Piano 1. Bodleian Library, Oxford, Mendelssohn Papers (see plate 5).[4] "C. 86: Ignaz Moscheles, loose sheets of music. Bequeathed by Helena Deneke, 1973: no. 3: F.M.B.'s cadenza for concerto for 2 pianos in E, 1823 (MS. Them. Cat. p. 24)."

Editorial Method

Mendelssohn's Holograph (FMB)

The first movement in its original form was 450 measures in length, with each manuscript page containing

113

approximately eight measures. The concerto is scored for a later Mozartian orchestra (see plate 1) of double winds (flutes, staff 1; oboes, staves 2 and 3; clarinets in A, staves 4 and 5; and bassoons, staves 6 and 7), double brass (horns in E, staff 8; and trumpets in E, staff 9), timpani (in E and B, one player, staff 10), strings (staves 11–13, and 18), and the two pianos (staves 14–17). The two solo parts are framed by the *Bassi* staff below and the higher strings above (see plate 2). Real five-part string writing is the exception rather than the rule in FMB, with no separate staff for the cello. Rather, within staff 18 verbal cues indicate which instruments are to play. Mendelssohn utilized this disposition for the solo instrument(s) in his four other juvenile concertos (Violin Concerto in D minor, 1822; Piano Concerto in A minor, 1822; Concerto for Violin and Piano in D minor, 1823; Concerto for Two Pianos and Orchestra in A-flat major, 1824). He altered this practice in the mature piano concertos (opp. 25 and 40) and the violin concerto (op. 64), with the solo part contained not within the orchestral score, but drafted separately.

FMB reveals the presence of several different hands, most prominently, of course, the adolescent composer's. This is shown by Mendelssohn's distinctive manner of forming the treble and bass clefs, seen on other, pre-1825 autographs. Also evident in this autograph, however, is the composer's mature script, seen in the equally distinctive manner of forming the treble and bass clefs. Both may be seen on p. 55 of the autograph, mm. 352[294]–353[295] (see plate 6). (Due to the unusual nature of this edition, measure numbers in the critical report will include those from the Köhler edition in brackets.) This new manner of forming the clefs is evident in the composer's first masterpieces, the Octet for Strings, op. 20 (composed in 1825), and the Overture to *A Midsummer Night's Dream*, op. 21 (composed in 1826).

The presence of Mendelssohn's later hand is evidence of his considerable efforts to revise the concerto, particularly the first movement. It appears that the revisions date from either 1829, around the time of Mendelssohn's performance of the concerto with Moscheles in London, or, just prior to his third visit to England, in late April 1833.[5]

In these areas of revision, replete with cross outs, scribbled-out measures, and penciled emendations, the composer has, in some cases, inserted revised readings in unused measures over the top of the crossed-out passages. In general, Mendelssohn's intentions following the revisions may be determined without difficulty; these are given in Karl-Heinz Köhler's edition of the concerto published in the *Leipziger Ausgabe*. Examining only Mendelssohn's holograph score, it is somewhat difficult to determine the composer's original intentions, due to the cross outs and scribbles over approximately 25 percent of the movement. However, by comparing Moscheles' manuscript copy of the concerto (M^1) and the set of copyist's parts (M^2) with Mendelssohn's autograph (FMB), the correct reading can be ascertained without difficulty. Utilizing all of these sources, I was confronted with few serious uncertainties. All significant discrepancies in markings between the three manuscripts are described in the critical notes.

At least three other hands are discernible in FMB, which Karl-Heinz Köhler tentatively identified as those of Carl Friedrich Zelter, Mendelssohn's composition teacher, Moscheles, and Ludwig Berger, Mendelssohn's piano teacher. A number of words are written on the autograph in English, possibly in the hand of Sir George Smart, the conductor of the Philharmonic Concerts, and the probable conductor of the performance in London with Moscheles in 1829.

The Moscheles Sources

As Mendelssohn's careful hand in FMB is perfectly legible, there are few questions of his intent. However, in the passages of revision, Mendelssohn's original intention is less clear, and sometimes completely obliterated. In these instances, I was assisted considerably by Moscheles's manuscript copy and set of parts.[6] While this copy is not dated, it most likely dates from approximately 1824 or shortly thereafter, when Moscheles first met the young Mendelssohn in Berlin.[7] M^1 corresponds almost exactly with FMB, except for occasional discrepancies in slurring, dynamics, and articulation. The disposition of instruments in M^1 is also slightly different than FMB, with the piano parts at the bottom of the score, and the four strings grouped together immediately above (compare plates 1 and 3). Because of these slight, but numerous discrepancies, it seems likely that Moscheles made his copy from yet another copy of the Mendelssohn autograph, now lost.[8] For example, a comparison of FMB (p. 59) with M^1 (pp. 38–39) shows that in FMB scalar runs are traded back and forth between Piano 1 and Piano 2, while in M^1 Moscheles keeps this passage entirely in Piano 1, with Piano 2 replicating the string parts (see mm. 389[331]–391[333]; compare plates 8 and 9).

It may be that many of these differences between FMB and M^1 stem from Moscheles's own, conscious or unconscious, editing during his copying of the manuscript. In this way, Mendelssohn's rather classical-looking score (i.e., with rather few indications of slurring, dynamics, and so forth) was transformed into a more Romantic-looking one. This may also account for the subtle changes in orchestration and voicing. Another factor that may come into play here is the nineteenth-century tendency to "correct" and "update" earlier music, or even that by contemporaries, a temptation to which Moscheles may have easily succumbed due to the fact that Mendelssohn was still an apprentice, teenaged, albeit extremely gifted, composer.

The final supplementary manuscript is a sketch for a cadenza to the first movement, also in Moscheles's hand, preserved in the Bodelian Library, Oxford (see plate 5). This cadenza draft was apparently produced following the rehearsal prior to the July 1829 performance of the concerto in London. As may be seen on p. 66 of FMB (see plate 7), the composer split measure 436[378] in half, apparently intending the original two half notes to become whole notes, and placed fermata signs over measure 437[379], intending the cadenza to be inserted here. The final tutti would then follow, beginning with measure 438[380].

Comparison of FMB and M¹

Because of the existence of M¹, we are permitted to see other elements added by Mendelssohn during the revision process. Many of these later additions concern dynamics, and these will be noted as necessary in the critical notes. But there are several points that can be made here.

In FMB the first movement originally began with the tempo designation *Allegro maestoso*. During revision, the composer altered the *maestoso* to become *moderato*, then changed his mind and struck through the *moderato*, and wrote *vivace* beneath it (see plate 1). M¹ confirms the first (*Allegro maestoso*) conception. At the solo entry at the recapitulation (p. 51; m. 322[264]), the piano 1 part reveals a temporary change of tempo to *Lento*, then *Adagio*. As the final tutti is reached (p. 66; m. 438[380]), Mendelssohn indicates an increase in tempo, *poco più Allegro*.

There is careful attention to dynamic markings throughout the score, with frequent changes of *p*, *f*, *ff*, etc., accents, *pizz.* and *arco*, and nuanced designations such as *espress.*, *dolce*, *dimin.*, *crescendo* and *decrescendo* (both as words and hairpins), *solo*, *soli*, and *tutti*. Dynamic markings are of three different types, and are distinguished as such in this edition. The first are those written by Mendelssohn in FMB, and which are also present in the M¹ copy; these are indicated by regular dynamics and hairpins. The second type are those which Mendelssohn did not include, but may be inferred by musical context; these are indicated by bold, roman type for dynamics, dashed hairpins and slurs, and square brackets around words or articulations. The third type are those added by Mendelssohn during the revision process, but not present in M¹; these are indicated by regular markings in parentheses.

As is typical in Mendelssohn's autographs, there are no measure numbers on the autograph. Page numbers have been entered into the upper right hand corner of every odd-numbered page, beginning with page one and ending with page sixty-seven. The two solo piano staves contain a tutti reduction, so that it was possible to play the entire concerto without the accompaniment of the orchestra (see plates 1 and 2). The tutti reduction is included in this edition, although it has been tacitly dropped in passages where it would make the solo part difficult to read. Instrumental cues (*Fl.*, *Fag.*, etc.) are written into the two solo piano parts. Also, verbal cues for the wind and brass parts are written into the string parts, presumably so the concerto could be performed with only string quartet accompaniment.

It is apparent that the score was utilized in performance, with rehearsal letters (*A* through *M*) inserted by a later hand throughout. Numerous minor corrections are indicated by the presence of scratched-out notes. More important are what appear to be a conductor's notes, found in several places: *c moll 6, 6/5* (pp. 26–27), *4 bar rest* (p. 49, mm. 316[258]–317[259]), *Cue* (p. 50, m. 320[262]), *In*, and *Stet* (pp. 52–54, mm. 352[294]–357[299]), *This*, and *Not This* (p. 55 [see plate 6]). A *Segno* indication (p. 65, m. 432[374]) implies a cut of six measures (to p. 66, m. 438[380]), eliminating the cadenza, called for by the fermatas throughout m. 437[378] (see plate 7). Other words, which I cannot decipher, are found at the following locations: bottom of p. 1, mm. 5–6; top of p. 27, m. 181; top of p. 30, m. 197[181]; p. 55, m. 357[299] and 362[304].

At the *Pianoforte 2 principale* entrance (p. 12, m. 92, staves 2–3), empty staves immediately above the part reveal sketches for alternative entry material.

Cross outs of complete pages are found in the following five locations (see table 4):

1. Transition section; pp. 14–15, following m. 102. Measures 103–8 are removed, excising statements of the primary theme from the soloists.
2. Secondary theme area; pp. 25–27. Following m. 172[166], measures 173–82 are removed, which confirm the new key (the dominant).
3. Second ritornello, approaching the development; pages 34–36, following m. 222[206]. Measures 223–38 are removed, involving confirmation of the new key (the dominant), and then transition to G major.
4. Development section; pp. 44–49. Following m. 286[254], measures 287–312 are removed. This is an area of sequential harmonic progression, which was revised and abridged substantially. Statements of the primary theme by the soloists have been scratched out, and substituted with statements of the second theme. This is the most extensive area of revision, revealing several layers, and difficult to puzzle out (see table 4).
5. Recapitulation section; pp. 52–54. Following m. 333[275], measures 334–52. Eighteen measures were removed initially, and then restored, with written emendations of *Stet* and *In* (p. 52, m. 334[276]) and *In* (p. 53, mm. 337[279]–339[281], and p. 54, mm. 345[287]–346[288]). The cross outs removed the restatement of a transition figure by the orchestra.

In this edition, the disposition of the right and left hand parts of both pianos has been tacitly adjusted so that the notes for each hand stay on their respective staves

Critical Notes

The critical notes provide rejected readings from FMB and comparisons of divergent readings between FMB and M¹. Because of the differences in measure numbering between FMB, M¹, and this edition, each critical note contains a reference to the Köhler edition in brackets and to the page in FMB in parentheses following the measure number of the edition. (Only one measure number appears for those passages cut in the Köhler edition.) For ease of comparison, the measure numbers of the Köhler edition are also included in the score in square brackets. Pitches are identified using the system in which middle C = c'. Instrument and other abbreviations used in the notes are as follows: Fl. = flute, Ob. = oboe, Cl. = clarinet, Bn. = bassoon, Hn. = horn, Tpt. = trumpet, Timp. = timpani, Vn. = violin, Va. = viola, Vc. = violoncello, Cb. = contrabass, Pn. = piano; ch = crescendo hairpin, dh = decrescendo hairpin, cdh = crescendo–decrescendo hairpins.

M. 1, (1), tempo *Allegro moderato*, as may be seen just below staff 18 in FMB; subsequently altered by Mendelssohn to *maestoso*, which was then crossed out and changed to *vivace*; M¹ has *Allegro maestoso*; FMB has (conductor's?) emendation: *Tutti*. Mm. 5–7, (1), Hn., crossed out; M¹ has the original reading. M. 19, Tpt., note 2, crossed out; not crossed out in M¹. Mm. 34–35, (5), Bn. 2, quarters c♮–d♮–d–d and whole d in FMB rev. M. 88, (11), Pn. 1, note 15, FMB has f♯′′′; M¹ has f𝄪′′′. M. 92, (12), FMB has sketches for two alternate readings. Mm. 93–103, (13), all parts, M¹ has many slurs not in FMB. M. 93, (13), Pn. 2, note 1, M¹ has accent not in FMB. M. 96, (13) Pn. 1, note 1, M¹ has accent not in FMB.

Mm. 103–8, (14–15), first of five areas of revision, crossed out; not crossed out in M¹. M. 109[103], (15), Fl., Cl. 2, Bn., Tpt., Vn., Va., note 1, pitches altered in FMB to make effective connection with m. 102 after the deletion of mm. 103–8. M. 114[108], (16), Pn. 1, b half note and two quarter notes crossed out; not crossed out in M¹. Mm. 119[113]–123[119], (17) Bn., and Hn., crossed out; not crossed out in M¹. Mm. 121[115]–122[116], (17), Pn. 1, original rhythm uncertain in FMB; M¹ has quarter notes in second half of both measures. M. 136[130], (19), Pn. 1, M¹ has cdh. Mm. 139[133]–141[135], (19–20), Hn., crossed out; not crossed out in M¹. Mm. 147[141]–150[144], (21), Bn., Hn., crossed out; not crossed out in M¹.

M. 154[148], (22), Pn. 2, bracketed notes from M¹. Mm. 154[148]–155[149], (22), Hn. 1, crossed out; not crossed out in M¹. M. 157[151], (22), M¹ has *un poco ritard.* not in FMB. M. 160[154], (23), Cl., Bn. 1, notes 2–3, crossed out; not crossed out in M¹; strings, notes 1–2, eighth note, eighth rest, eighth note, eighth rest in FMB rev. Mm. 173–82, (25–27), second of five areas of revision, crossed out; not crossed out in M¹. M. 179, (26), (conductor's?) penciled emendation, *c moll 6* (i. e., C major first inversion = Neapolitan ♮II of B major, the key of the dominant). M. 180, (27), (conductor's?) penciled emendation, *6/5* (i. e., a♯ diminished seventh chord, first inversion = vii°⁶₅ of B). M. 181, (27), sketch for Pn. 2 figuration between Pn. 1 staves. M. 183[167], (27), note 1, original notes scratched out in almost all parts and new notes added to agree with the cut of ten measures beginning in m. 173; M¹ has the original notes. M. 196[180], (30), Pn. 1, LH, note 1, M¹ has *ff*. Mm. 197[181]–200[184], (30), Bn., Hn., crossed out; not crossed out in M¹.

M. 200[184], (30), Pn. 2, RH, note 1 is a. Mm. 207[191]–210[194], (32), FMB has dynamics significantly altered from those found in M¹. M. 209[193], (32), Vc./Cb., *pp*. Mm. 210[194]–211[195], (32), Tpt., partially crossed out; not crossed out in M¹. M. 212[196], (33), Ob. 1, Bn., altered; M¹ has the reading produced by the alteration. M. 213[197], (33), Cl. 1, altered; M¹ has the reading produced by the alteration; Vn. 1, note 2, d♯′ in both FMB and M¹. Mm. 213[197]–216[200], (33), Tpt. 1, altered; M¹ has the original reading. Mm. 215[199]–217[201], (33), Cl., altered; M¹ has the original reading. M. 218[202], (34), Fl., altered; M¹ has the reading produced by the alteration. M. 219, (34), Tpt., crossed out; not crossed out in M¹. Mm. 223–38, (34–36), third of five areas of revision; not crossed out in M¹. M. 239[207], all parts, note 1, pitches altered in almost every part to make effective connection with m. 222 after deletion of mm. 223–38; M¹ has the original reading.

M. 251[219], (38), Fl. 1, altered; M¹ has the reading produced by the alteration. Mm. 259[227]–260[228], (39–40), Pn. 2, crossed out; M¹ has the original reading. Mm. 263[231]–264[232], (40), Pn. 2, crossed out; M¹ has the original reading. M. 265[233], (40), Bn. 2, crossed out; M¹ has the original reading. Mm. 269[237]–286[254], (41–44), substantial revisions in almost every part; M¹ has the original reading. Mm. 287[255]–312[280], (44–49), fourth of five areas of revision, entirely crossed out and at different times, reflecting several layers of revision; not crossed out in M¹. Mm. 292a–c, crossed out in FMB; not present in M¹. Mm. 294–96 and 298–304, (46–47), Vc., bracketed notes from M¹.

M. 313[255]–315[257], (49), Ob. 2, Cl. 1, and Cl. 2, see example 1. Mm. 313[255]–316[258], (49), ♮ on D's in Bn. 2, Pn. 1, Pn. 2, and strings. Mm. 316[258]–317[259], (49), (conductor's?) penciled emendation, *4 bar rest*; not in M¹. M. 320[262], (50), (conductor's?) penciled emendation, *Cue*; not in M¹. M. 325[267], (51), Pn. 1 and 2, M¹ makes the re-entrances one measure each, instead of being contained all in one measure, as they are in FMB. Mm. 334[276]–361[303], (52–54), fifth of five areas of revision, crossed out and at different times, reflecting several layers of revision; not crossed out in M¹. M. 334[276], (52), (conductor's?) penciled emendation, *In*, and *Stet*; not in M¹. Mm. 338[280]–339[318], (53), (conductor's?) penciled emendation, *In*; not in M¹.

Mm. 364[306]–365[307], (56), Hn., crossed out; not crossed out in M¹. Mm. 375[317]–376[318], (57), Hn., strings, crossed out; not crossed out in M¹. M. 383[325], (58), Vc./Cb., note 3, FMB has half note c♯. M. 389[331], (59), Cl., Bn. 1, altered; M¹ has the reading produced by the alteration. Mm. 389[331]–392[333], (59), Pn. 1 and Pn. 2, substantial differences in the disposition of notes (see plates 8 and 9). M. 395[337], (60), Vn. 2, M¹ has *p*. M. 397[339], (60), Va., note 1, M¹ has *p*. M. 398[340], (60), Bassi, note 1, M¹ has *p*. M. 399[341], (60), Va., altered; M¹ has the reading produced by the alteration. Mm. 399[341]–400[342], (60), Pn. 1, LH, bracketed notes from M¹.

Example 1. Mendelssohn, Concerto for Two Pianos and Orchestra in E Major (1823), reading of mm. 313[255]–315[257] from M¹.

M. 406[348], (61), Bn. 1, altered; M¹ has the reading produced by the alteration. M. 414[356], (62), Vn. 2, altered; M¹ has the reading produced by the alteration. Mm. 422[363]–424[366], (64), Pn. 1, altered;. M¹ has the reading produced by the alteration. Mm. 424[366]–425[367], (64), strings, whole notes without tremolos in M¹. Mm. 424[366]–426[368], (64), strings, accents (Vn. 1) and tremolos not in M¹. M. 428[370], (65), M¹ has *f*. Mm. 432[374]–437[379], (65–66), a *Segno* indication, which implies a cut of six measures, eliminating the cadenza and following tutti, called for by the fermatas throughout m. 437[379]; these measures (432[374]–437[379]) are not in M¹. M. 436[378], (66), added barline in FMB, implying that this measure becomes two measures in preparation for the cadenza in m. 437[379] at the added fermatas. M. 437[379], (66), a *Segno* indication, signifying the end of the six-measure cut begun in m. 432[374]; not in M¹. Mm. 438[380]–439[381], (66), M¹ has *Più Allegro*.

Notes

1. The second movement is not dated; the third is inscribed *d. 17 Oct. 1823*. Mendelssohn had this concerto bound in this volume, along with other compositions from around this time. Following the composer's death, Mendelssohn's manuscripts remained in the possession of his descendants. In 1878, upon completion of Julius Rietz's edition of the forty-one-volume Mendelssohn *Gesamtausgabe*, the composer's manuscripts were given by Mendelssohn's heirs to the Prussian government, in exchange for the creation of the Felix Mendelssohn-Bartholdy-Stiftung, which awards two annual scholarships and other support for the musical arts. The manuscripts were deposited in the Königliche Bibliothek where they remained until approximately 1940, when the contents of the library was removed from Berlin as a safety precaution during the Second World War. Following the war, because the Mendelssohn autographs were returned to the Deutsche Staatsbibliothek in the communist sector of Berlin, Western scholars were able to study these manuscripts only with considerable difficulty. Shortly after reunification of the two Germanys in 1989, however, the manuscripts became readily available to all interested persons. (For a brief history of this situation, see Dominick Sackmann, "Classical Music—A State Secret," trans. Susan Gillespie, *Musical Quarterly* 82 (1998): 160–89.) I am particularly grateful to Dr. Hans Günter-Klein, of the Musikabteilung mit Mendelssohn Archiv in the Staatsbibliothek zu Berlin Preußischer Kulturbesitz for his considerable assistance with the Mendelssohn autographs.

I am grateful for the research grant awarded by the Brigham Young University College of Fine Arts and Communications, which permitted me to examine both the Mendelssohn autograph and the Moscheles copy at the Deutsche Staatsbibliothek zu Berlin in June 1998.

2. See R. Larry Todd, "The Unfinished Mendelssohn," in *Mendelssohn and His World*, ed. R. Larry Todd (Princeton, N.J.: Princeton University Press, 1991), 163. I am grateful to Professor Todd for his assistance with deciphering this phrase, which has been partially cut off during rebinding.

3. The diary entry to which the librarian is referring states: "22. Juni (Friday) . . . Für Abend liess ich Fräul. Schilling u. Schwalbe Mendelssohn's Doppel-Concert mit Quartett-Begleitung probiren . . . Den Schluss (vor der Abend-Unterhaltung im Leipziger Conservatorium) bildete das obengenannte Doppel-Concert welches ich aus einer mir geliehenen Abschrift (Moritz) in Partitur gesetz habe" (22 June [Friday]. For the evening I listened to Fräulein Schilling and Schwalbe's attempt at the Mendelssohn Double Concerto with quartet accompaniment . . . The Finale [of the evening concert in the Leipzig Conservatory] was the above mentioned Double Concerto which I had copied in score from a copy lent to me [Moritz]). My translation.

The "Moritz" in question is in all probability Moscheles's friend, the publisher Moritz Schlesinger. The quote is found in a catalogue published in 1911 by the Berlin antiquarian dealer Leo Liepmannsohn, advertising the sale of Moscheles' copy of the concerto. Liepmannsohn noted that Moscheles's son Felix had furnished the dealer with this quote from his father's diary. I am grateful to Ingeborg Heussner for this information.

4. For a full citation, see note 10 to the introduction.

5. For more on the revisions to the concerto, see Stephan D. Lindeman, "Mendelssohn and Moscheles: Two Composers, Two Pianos, Two Scores, One Concerto," *The Musical Quarterly* 83 (1999): 51–74.

6. Following Moscheles's death in 1870, his manuscript copy of the Mendelssohn Concerto for Two Pianos and Orchestra in E major, along with other manuscripts from his sizeable collection of autographs, including works by J. S. Bach, Beethoven, and others, was sold. It became part of the collection of Betty Wolffheim, of Berlin, and was donated to the, then, Preußischer Staatsbibliothek in 1934 (see Karl-Heinz Köhler, "Zum vorliegenden Band," *Felix Mendelssohn Bartholdy: Konzert für zwei Klavier und Orchester E-Dur*, Leipziger Ausgabe der Werke Felix Mendelssohn Bartholdy, Ser. II, Bd. 4, [Leipzig: Deutscher Verlag für Musik, 1960; repr. 1971]). After World War II, it formed part of the collection in West Berlin, where it remained until reunification. It has now been returned to the Musikabteilung mit Mendelssohn Archiv.

7. Moscheles describes a double concerto that Mendelssohn showed him at this time, in *Moscheles Leben*, 65.

8. It is possible that other copies of the work were made; see Marcia J. Citron, ed. and trans., *The Letters of Fanny Hensel to Felix Mendelssohn* (Stuyvesant, N.Y., 1987), 10–11, 26–27, with reference to Fanny's copying of the A-flat major concerto for two pianos.

Recent Researches in the Music of the Nineteenth and Early Twentieth Centuries
Rufus Hallmark, general editor

Vol.	Composer: *Title*
1–2	Jan Ladislav Dussek: *Selected Piano Works*
3–4	Johann Nepomuk Hummel: *Piano Concerto, Opus 113*
5	*One Hundred Years of Eichendorff Songs*
6	Etienne-Nicolas Méhul: *Symphony No. 1 in G Minor*
7–8	*Embellished Opera Arias*
9	*The Nineteenth-Century Piano Ballade: An Anthology*
10	*Famous Poets, Neglected Composers: Songs to Lyrics by Goethe, Heine, Mörike, and Others*
11	Charles-Marie Widor: *Symphonie I in C Minor*
12	Charles-Marie Widor: *Symphonie II in D Major*
13	Charles-Marie Widor: *Symphonie III in E Minor*
14	Charles-Marie Widor: *Symphonie IV in F Minor*
15	Charles-Marie Widor: *Symphonie V in F Minor*
16	Charles-Marie Widor: *Symphonie VI in G Minor*
17	Charles-Marie Widor: *Symphonie VII in A Minor*
18	Charles-Marie Widor: *Symphonie VIII in B Major*
19	Charles-Marie Widor: *Symphonie gothique*
20	Charles-Marie Widor: *Symphonie romane*
21	Archduke Rudolph of Austria: *Forty Variations on a Theme by Beethoven for Piano; Sonata in F Minor for Violin and Piano*
22	Fanny Hensel: *Songs for Pianoforte, 1836–1837*
23	*Anthology of Goethe Songs*
24	Walter Rabl: *Complete Instrumental Chamber Works*
25	Stefano Pavesi: *Dies irae concertato*
26	Franz Liszt: *St. Stanislaus*
27	George Frederick Pinto: *Three Sonatas for Pianoforte with Violin*
28	Felix Mendelssohn: *Concerto for Two Pianos and Orchestra in E Major (1823): Original Version of the First Movement*